Aboard the Portland:
A History of the Northwest Steamers

Library of Congress Cataloging-in-Publication Data

Harrison, Rebecca

Aboard the Portland: A History of the Northwest Steamers

FIRST EDITION

CreateSpace is a trademark of Amazon Technologies Inc. This book is not written, published, or endorsed by CreateSpace or Amazon affiliates.

While every effort has been made to be accurate, the author assumes no responsibility for errors.

Cover layout by the author
Front cover photograph is of the *Portland* sternwheeler.
Photograph is from the Oregon Maritime Museum collection.
Back cover photograph of the author is from Lifetouch Church Directories and Portraits.

Printed and Bound in the United States of America on acid free paper.

Aboard the Portland:
A History of the Northwest Steamers

Rebecca Harrison

Also by Rebecca Harrison

Child Abuse: A Guide for Teachers and Professionals
Co-authored with Jean Edwards

*Deep Dark and Dangerous: On the Bottom with
the Northwest Salvage Divers*

Images of America: Portland's Maritime History
Co-authored with Daniel Cowan

Images of America: Canby (To be published 08/2016)
Co-authored with Daniel Cowan

TABLE OF CONTENTS

Acknowledgements | iii

When did the first steamboats travel to the Northwest?
    From Covered Wagons to the Water | 1
    From Fur Trappers to Shanghaiing | 9
    From Ships to Paddlewheels | 11

One Man, Many Sternwheelers | 25

The Life of a Sidewheeler: the *Gazelle* | 37

Minnie Hill: the First Woman Steamboat Captain
             on the West Coast | 47

The Steamers *M. F. Henderson* and *Henderson* | 71

The Steamboat *Georgiana* | 79

The First *Portland* Steamers | 87

Aboard the *Portland (II)* | 91
    Profiles of Two *Portland* Captains | 99

Appendices
    A: The Oregon Maritime Museum | 117
    B: *Portland* steamer sternwheeler technical data | 118
    C: Some of the early Northwest steamboats | 123
    D: The Shaver Transportation Company | 168

Bibliography | 169

Early in the 1800s, sternwheelers transported goods and people between Portland, Salem, Albany, and even as far as Eugene. The City of Salem was built in 1875 and worked on the rivers for 20 years. (Larry Barber Collection)

Samuel Langhorne Clemens was an American humorist, journalist, lecturer, and novelist who earned international fame for his travel narratives, especially *The Innocents Abroad* (1869), *Roughing It* (1872), and *Life on the Mississippi* (1883). Clemens was best known under his pseudonym Mark Twain, the famous author of *The Adventures of Tom Sawyer* and *Adventures of Huckleberry Finn.*

Clemens began working as a cub pilot on Mississippi River steamboats and earned his steamboat pilot license in 1859. He then worked as a pilot until 1861, when the American Civil War stopped all river traffic. In 1862 he began working as a reporter for the *Virginia City Territorial Enterprise* in Nevada. It was in 1863 that Samuel Clemens began using the pen name Mark Twain, a term used for measuring the depth of a river with a weighted line. Crewmen used the phrase "mark twain" to signal that the boat was in water deep enough, two fathoms, to pass through safely. From there on, most of Mark Twain's stories included a steamboat or two.

ACKNOWLEDGEMENTS

A great deal of the facts and information for this book were accumulated through personal interviews and correspondence with the volunteers at the Oregon Maritime Museum, located on the steam sternwheeler *Portland*, moored on the Willamette River in Portland, Oregon, USA. It was their idea and encouragement to create these pages of maritime history including the design, restoration, and maintenance of one of the last steam-powered sternwheel tugboats to be built in the United States.

I made every effort to make sure that the information covered in my book is up to date, current, and accurate as of the date of printing – 2016.

I owe much gratitude to the river pilots, maritime volunteers and their families who shared their experiences with me, personal photographs, and assisted me with support in the technical aspects of the construction, operations, and maintenance of boats in general, but especially the *Portland*. Special credits are due to these maritime folks:

Bill Fishback, Gloria Holman, Captain Jack Taylor, Robert Woolsey, Ron Youngman, and the late Captain Dale Russell.

My thanks also goes to Peter Marsh, outdoor & nautical writer and boat builder, for Larry Barber's private collection of notes, published articles and photographs. I have a special appreciation to the late Herb Beals, historian, and author, for his help on portions of the history used in my book.

In addition, I am grateful to my husband, Daniel S. Cowan, who answered most of my grammatical questions, edited the majority of my work and layout, gave me a book title, and scanned the pictures displayed in this book.

Rebecca Harrison

The Multnomah was built in East Portland in 1885. She was meticulously fine in all her arrangements. She had no timbers except her deck beams and the frame upon which her engine and machinery rested; she was as strong as the iron and oak in her hull. Assembled for the run from Portland to Oregon City, this sternwheeler was one of the best boats on the river for her time. Here she is at upper dock on the 4th Street Dock in Oregon City.

The Multnomah worked on both the Columbia and Willamette Rivers until 1899. She was then transferred north to Puget Sound, Washington. Under her new owners, the S. Willey Navigation Company, she made regular runs from Olympia to places along the Puget Sound.

On October 28, 1911, the Multnomah was working in dense fog in Elliot Bay, Washington, and was crashed into by the steamer Iroquois, sinking in 240 feet of water.

(Larry Barber Collection)

WHEN DID THE FIRST STEAMBOATS TRAVEL TO THE NORTHWEST?

FROM COVERED WAGONS TO THE WATER

The viceroy of Mexico sent two ships in 1542 to explore what is now Northern California. Juan Rodrigo Cabrillo, a Portuguese captain organized the journey, while Spanish explorer, Bartolome Ferrer (also known as Bartolome Ferrelo) worked as the pilot. Cabrillo's expedition was the first exploration of the West Coast. The men continued north on the Pacific Ocean, experiencing a harrowing storm which tossed the ship all the way to Oregon's midpoint, but few records were kept of this adventure. The Oregon coast was first noted as early as 1543 when Ferrer sailed up the west coast of what would later become the United States of America. He seems to have sighted it near the Rogue River at about 42 ½ degrees north latitude.

According to some accounts, Englishman Francis Drake stopped along the Oregon coast in 1579. It was not until 1774, long after the Russian expeditions of Vitus Jonassen Bering and Aleksei Ilyich Chirikov to the southeastern lands of Alaska in 1741, that it became of interest to Europe. The Spanish sent several excursions to explore and map the coastline from California to Alaska. Even though the Columbia River estuary was discovered and mapped by Bruno de Hezeta (Heceta) from Spain in 1775, his surveys were very sketchy. He could not enter the river due to the lack of his scurvy ridden crew's ability to take on the rough conditions of the river bar.

Soon the British had a hunger for exploring the unknown Pacific Coast. In 1776, Captain Cook accepted the challenge of leading an excursion to survey the Pacific Northwest, primarily in search of a northwest passage. For years, it was believed a navigable waterway existed across North America from the Atlantic to the Pacific Ocean. Many explorers had searched the Atlantic Coast for such a passage, but to no avail.

In the same year the American colonies declared their independence, Captain Cook left Britain with two ships, the *Resolution* and the *Discover*. The expedition rounded Africa and entered the Pacific. By 1778, Captain James Cook was still on his exploration and desperately needed fresh water, supplies, and the ships were in need of repair. He sighted the Oregon coast, but he found no landing or harbor. Storms were breaking the water, so the ships proceeded north, missing the mouth of the Columbia River. His voyage did however open the doors to the Oregon coast; he mapped two Oregon capes, Perpetua and Foulweather. Soon after his charting, vessels were sailing over the waters with fur traders.

Many stories were told from ships and their crews bragging about trading many cheap knickknacks from home for sea otter pelts from the indigenous peoples of the Pacific Northwest Coast and the money they made selling them in China. By 1785, the west coast was bustling with exploratory ships in pursuit of profitable skins.

One noted exploration of these waters was by Captain Robert Gray in 1792. On his second voyage to the Northwest coastline, Captain Gray hoped that he could barter with the native Americans for prime pelts. Once he returned, he expected to make a sizable profit. He was able to cross the bar and examined a magnificent river he named the Columbia. Following that same year, British explorer Lt. William Broughton, a skipper of the little sloop *Chatham*, which accompanied George Vancouver's party, entered the Columbia River and ventured about one hundred miles upriver. He was the first white explorer to log a passage of the reach and he became enamored with it. He called it "The Friendly Reach" because many native Americans paddled along with him in their dugouts as far as the mouth of the Willamette. These explorations led many new travelers and entrepreneurs to settle along the rivers in the Oregon Country.

The North West Company, headquartered in Montreal, was a business created for trapping and trading furs in the eastern Canadian provinces; it was established in 1779. It pushed westward across the continent in the 1780s and 1790s. In 1793, fur trader and geographer Alexander McKenzie led an expedition across the Canadian Rockies and down the Fraser River to the Pacific Coast. His party was the first to cross North America above the Rio Grande River. David Thompson, another North West Company dealer, successfully followed the Columbia River from its headwaters to its mouth in 1811.

One of President Thomas Jefferson's goals was to locate a direct and attainable water passage across the land for the trade and commerce with Asia (the Northwest Passage.) Jefferson wanted to declare U.S. sovereignty over the native Americans along the Mississippi River, as well as getting a precise appraisal of the resources available in the recently completed Louisiana Purchase.

In 1805, President Thomas Jefferson sent Meriwether Lewis & William Clark to secure the claim of the land purchased from France for the United States and map the northwest. After crossing the Rocky Mountains, their journey reached the Pacific Ocean in what is now Oregon (which lay beyond the nation's new boundaries) in November. They returned in 1806, with a vast amount of information about the region and its waterways.

As the fur trade kept expanding and new businesses kept appearing from the east, the Pacific Fur Company, founded by Jacob Astor, a very successful East Coast investor, was created in 1811. With a direct river route to the ocean, the town of Astoria was established in the most northwestern corner of the Oregon Country. During the War of 1812, the American post in Astoria was captured by the British and handed over to the North West Company; they renamed it Fort George. The land was later returned to United States ownership as Britain agreed on a "joint occupancy" for the Oregon Territory in 1818. By then the Company had several trading posts along the lower Columbia River.

During all these years of expansion and population growth, both the Columbia and the Willamette Rivers were a cruel challenge to cross with their unforgiving rapids and their deep swelling waters. Still, many folks kept traveling across the Midwestern plains to settle in the rugged northwest, bringing their hopes and desires to the new land. By the time many settlers arrived at The Dalles, a bustling town in the northeastern section of the Oregon Country, they decided the Columbia River was the most practical route through the Cascades and Coast Range. (As harsh as the mountains were to cross, they chose to raft the river versus the strenuous hike around Mt. Hood.)

Farmers, explorers, and fur trappers of the North West Company relied on the waterway (even with its fierce rapids and shallow rock filled basins) for the quickest route to and from trading posts and interior forts. By using an exhausting struggle of poling and paddling their heavily loaded canoes, the men would transport their goods and services.

Commercial ships soon entered the Columbia River via the Pacific Ocean. While going upriver, these rugged shipping ferries were filled with furs, people, and supplies. The Hudson's Bay Company had already secured a fur monopoly for all of British Northern America after merging with the North West Company in 1821. Dr. John McLoughlin worked for the Hudson Bay Company in Ontario, Canada. In 1824, he was appointed Chief Factor of the Columbia District and was sent to Astoria. Fort Vancouver became the principal depot of the Hudson's Bay Company, located west of the Rocky Mountains.

When Dr. McLoughlin arrived at Astoria, he was dismayed by the rough wooden layout where he was expected to run a business. Being so used to taking on projects, such as the merging of the North West Company and Hudson's Bay, he designated a new location, built a fort at Belle Vue Point, and named it Fort Vancouver (now Vancouver, Washington). He chose that location because it had good soil and was at the junction of three fur trade routes through the Columbia, Willamette, and Cowlitz Rivers.

When it was complete, Fort Vancouver was about 750 feet long and 450 feet wide with a stockade about 20 feet high. The northwest corner had two 12-pound cannons and the center had many 18-pounders. Inside were accommodations for married officers, Dr. McLoughlin's house, a community kitchen, a washhouse, and other small residences. It sat just four hundred yards from the north banks of the Columbia River and about one hundred miles east of its mouth. The post was open for business on March 19, 1825.

The Willamette Falls   (Photo by Rebecca Harrison)

By the year 1843, more than 800 eager pioneers had made their way to the Oregon Country. As more people came to trap the rampant wildlife for their meat and fur, plant new farmlands and orchards, the number quickly exceeded 30,000. Soon over 200,000 settlers had come out west on the Oregon Trail.

After resigning from the Hudson's Bay Company in 1846, Dr. McLoughlin took his family to settle south. The Willamette Valley had become a popular destination for settlers, so businesses were booming. Dr. McLoughlin opened a shop where he sold food and farming supplies. As his profits grew, Dr. McLoughlin donated a segment of his land claim at Willamette Falls to be established as Oregon City. This area was located between the earlier location of native American fisheries (tribal fishing waters) and the trading towns of Clackamas Rapids and Willamette Falls.

Oregon City became the trade center between the Pacific coast and inland sellers. It was the first community pioneers saw after leaving the Midwest. The river trade, houses, churches, and small businesses were a welcoming site to these trail worn explorers. The new residents learned how to use the power of Willamette Falls from the native Americans as their source of water. Soon there were many dairy farms, orchards, textile mills, and developing lumber mills, boatyards and flour mills.

Oregon became a U.S. territory in 1848 and Oregon City, the business and governmental center of the region, was named its capital. Dr. McLoughlin served as mayor of Oregon City in 1851, winning 44 of 66 votes. Dr. McLoughlin was a key player in establishing the maritime businesses along the Clackamas and Willamette Rivers near Oregon City. In 1857, Dr. McLoughlin died; his grave is located beside his home overlooking downtown Oregon City.

Overall, the Columbia River waterways covered the Pacific Northwest south of the 49th parallel of latitude and shared the territory north of the 49th with Canadian rivers. The Columbia was the life flow for all native Americans who lived along her shore and made it possible for all the upcoming northwest communities to flourish and hasten trade.

The freight steam sternwheeler, Cascade, built in 1864, was traveling on the upper end of the Columbia River in 1867. (Oregon Maritime Museum Collection)

The Columbia River was then, and still is, the main waterway for nautical transportation. It is the largest river in the Pacific Northwest region of the United States; it drains a 259,000 square mile basin that includes territory in seven states (Oregon, Washington, Idaho, Montana, Nevada, Wyoming, and Utah) and one Canadian province. The Columbia River is the most important environmental force in the Pacific Northwest region of the United States. It streams for more than 1,200 miles, from the base of the Canadian Rockies in southeastern British Columbia to the Pacific Ocean at Astoria, Oregon, and Ilwaco, Washington. The river marks nearly the entire border between Oregon and Washington. Much of the river in early history was divided into three main lengths:

* The *lower river* includes the flow from Astoria upriver to where the Willamette River runs into the Columbia. The lower river incorporated the run up the Columbia River Gorge from the mouth of the Willamette to the portage and later, the locks at the Cascade Rapids.

* The *middle river* began at the top of the Cascades to The Dalles, where another set of whitewater rapids began, called Celilo Falls, which needed another much longer portage.

* The *upper river,* meaning the direction from Celilo Village, at the top of Celilo Falls, to Wallula Gap, where it reaches the mouth of the Snake River.

The passenger boat, Beaver is on the Columbia River in the 1860s.
(Oregon Maritime Museum Collection)

Almost thirty years after the famous explorers Lewis and Clark put their canoes into these same waters, the sound of a steam whistle resonated across the water framing the power of the mighty Columbia River. Winter weather conditions around the Columbia were normally mild so most boats could run all year. When ice formed on the water, it was usually only of a short-term duration. In these latitudes, it was practical to protect an idle steamboat from the damage created by the breaking up of ice without resorting to pulling the hull up onshore for the winter.

As the steamboats entered the Columbia River, it was still an awkward journey for settlers to travel for goods and supplies. Before the railroads came out west, explorers heading from the growing city of Portland to the coast or north generally traveled by the Columbia River. This route was like a natural maze. One started by taking a steamboat up to the Cascades, where rapids blocked the river to all upstream traffic and made downstream traffic very risky. The next step was to take a portage railroad (first hauled by mules, later by steam engines), which progressed to the top of the Cascades. At this point one would then board another steamboat to go on up river to The Dalles, where the course would be repeated for a 13 mile trip around Celilo Falls and on past more fast moving water upriver, which like the Columbia, at this stage, was unnavigable both upstream and downstream.

This is the second *Harvest Queen* built along the Columbia River. *(The first was crafted in Celilo in 1878, and was part of a fleet of seven steamers. The others were Dalles City, Maria, Regulator, Sadie B, Sarah Dixon, and Water Witch. She was dismantled in 1879.)*

This Harvest Queen was the Oregon Railway and Navigation Co.'s new steam sternwheeler. Peter Carsten built her in 1900, on the Lower Columbia River. She worked until 1927. The sternwheeler was 187 feet long, 585 tons, with a 39.8 beam and a light 6 to 8 foot draft. (Oregon Maritime Museum Collection)

FROM FUR TRAPPERS TO SHANGHAIING

In 1852, settlers found gold dust in the ocean sands in the southern Oregon territory. By 1853, thousands of eager pioneers were washing gold out of the black sand along the seashore south of Coos Bay. Gold facilitated many of Oregon's towns. Portland was officially "founded" in 1843. The first transportation system in Portland was the Columbia and Willamette Rivers. The riverfront was quickly inhabited with sailing ships and steamboats.

Every day, the steamers from San Francisco were filled with gold miners ready to discover their fortune. Throughout 1861 and 1862, the *Oregonian* newspaper ran several lead articles with gold hunting accounts and success stories in Eastern Oregon.

Unfortunately, by 1870, along with the miners, traders and marketers came the evil practice of maritime slavery, known as crimping or shanghai. This cruel and unmerited practice would continue for the next 45 or 50 years, leaving a mark on the names of both Portland and Astoria. The shanghaiers called themselves "sailor's boardinghouse keepers" but everyone else called them "crimps." Crimping (a Dutch word for a holding pen for fish) was an underhanded waterfront business in any main harbor town, including Portland and Astoria. Crimps ran sailor's boarding houses, saloons, marine supply stores, and brothels all in efforts to get the sailor intoxicated, sign a contract, and go aboard a ship. It was easier to load a drunken sailor than to fight with a sober man who did not want to go out to sea, so sometimes the crimps laced the whiskey with laudanum (a type of morphine). They were paid per sailor, referred to as "blood money," and often collected their fee from the sailor's pay in advance. These gratuities ranged anywhere from $30 to $120 a head. Often, the victims were enticed to take a tour to see the beautiful harbor. The men drunkenly signed a contract, being told it was the "passenger list. " Once signed, the future seamen were handcuffed, or threatened with guns, and taken onto the vessel. After they were transferred on board a ship and deep out to the sea, they were told what had happened and that they were now deckhands for as long as the crew decided to keep them. The shanghaied men were kicked and beaten into a painful submission. The law couldn't do much against this as the men did sign those contracts.

Portland soon became one of the most popular ports in the world for this unsavory practice of "shanghaiing" baffled men, marketing them through an underground network known as the Shanghai Tunnels, and selling them as slave hands on merchant ships. There were men like Irishman, Joseph "Bunco" Kelly, a proprietor infamous for kidnapping young men and selling them to ship captains. Kelly had tried and failed to keep a deceitful boardinghouse, but he profited stalking the streets for young targets. By 1890, many bar owners and hotel operators depended on this shanghai trade to maintain their businesses, and Kelly was one of the best. Kelly would deliver his drunken victims outfitted as ABs (able-bodied mariners) to waiting ships and collect his pay on the foredeck by ruthless captains before the men could sober up.

Kelly often boasted that he could gather a full crew in less than 12 hours. One of the most popular stories told about Kelly was when a ship captain challenged him. That night Kelly spied upon a group who had stumbled upon the open cellar of a mortuary. Thinking the cellar was a part of the Snug Harbor Pub, the men each guzzled containers of embalming fluid, which they mistook for liquor. When Kelly found them, several had died and others were dying. Claiming the dead were merely unconscious from too much drink, Kelly sold all 22 to the captain whose ship sailed before he found out he had paid for dead men.

Another story about Kelly was the time he delivered a dime store Indian heavily wrapped in blankets to a ship. When the captain learned the next morning that his new crew member was a wooden statue, he became so angry that he threw it overboard. Two men operating a dredge nearly 60 years later claimed to have recovered it.

Astoria was one of the West Coast's most prominent shipping ports and a very easy place for crimps as well. It was also the town that contributed to the collapse of the trade after the story of a man nearly dying after being shanghaied and jumping ship ran in *The Astorian* newspaper. The public rioted against this practice. Once it was outlawed, Astoria began to stabilize with an aggressive police force that removed the vigilante system for these crimes.

Shanghaiing ended partially because of steamboats. Labor-intensive ferries and schooners were giving way to the smaller staffed steamships, and it was no longer necessary to crimp up a line of captured crewmen. These vessels were much safer and more relaxing for the required work.

The end of shanghaiing in Portland, as well as the United States, is credited to Andrew Furuseth, president of the International Seaman's Union. He worked diligently for years trying to stop the enforced servitude of kidnapped sailors. By 1915, with his effort, the federal government finally acted by passing the Seaman's Act, providing the merchant marine with rights similar to those gained by factory workers. Once this took place, the crimps lost their hold.

Steamship captains would now just hire workers directly without the use of boarding masters. This simplified the time hunting for a crew and made the work appealing for honest pay. There still were a few crimps stalking along the harbors and captive men "enlisted" on a number of international ships as late as 1930.

FROM SHIPS TO PADDLEWHEELS

With the successful sailing of the first steamer in 1801, ships were no longer subjected to the frightful winds and currents of the waterways. Steamships proved to be more navigable and sturdier than sailing vessels. (A steamboat or steamship, sometimes called a steamer, is a vessel in which the primary method of momentum is steam power, typically driving propellers or paddlewheels. A propeller is the most common propulsion on ships, using the motion of the water causes a force to move the boat.) Many types of steamboats were making their way on inland rivers, such as propeller driven, sidewheeler, and sternwheeler. The river steamers were shallow of draft, seldom drawing over two or three feet to avoid rocks. Their hulls were flat bottomed, turning up at the chines to the deck levels. While steamers were rapidly changing to fit the needs of the waters, the growth from sidewheel to screw propulsion was mild. From 1850 to 1889, at least 50 steamers, both sidewheelers and sternwheelers, were constructed in Oregon City, Linn City (West Linn), Milwaukie, and New Era.

The sidewheeler *Multnomah* made her first trial run in August of 1851 above the Willamette Falls in Oregon City. She had been built in New Jersey. She was made out of oak staves, which were two inches thick, and had the width and length of ordinary boat plank, bound with hoops made of bar iron, keyed up on the gunwales. Her hull was barrel-shaped, held in shape by iron hoops. This made it needless to caulk the works. Her funnel was equipped with a spark arrester. The craft was 108 feet in length, built with quality machinery.

To get to Oregon, she was dismantled and each piece was packed and shipped in numbered sections to Oregon City on the bark *Success*. During this time, the locks at Willamette Falls had not yet been developed, so it was questionable if a boat could be built above the falls, but it was decided to assemble her in Canemah. (Canemah was the last stop upriver of a portage roadway that circled around the Willamette Falls.)

On her trial run in June of 1851, her engines were tested for durability. She was then sent out in August over to Cressman's Bar, a location about 20 miles downriver from the town of Salem. The water was too shallow at Cressman's for the *Multnomah*, which only needed 18 inches of depth; she could not easily get through without hitting the bottom. She continued another 5 miles upstream to Matthew's Landing where the water was again too low.

The *Multnomah* needed deeper water to be useful, but to move her from the falls, she was lined over to the lower river. (Lining was the term used for hooking a cable to the boat and a point on shore, and hauling on the cable by using the steamer's capstan to move it upward and through the rapids. This system could also be used to take the vessel over rapids and short falls.)

The Albany was a stern wheel driven steamboat that ran on the Wilmette River from 1868 to 1875. This steamer was the first of the two that were named Albany that worked on this river. (Oregon Maritime Museum Collection)

The sidewheeler Multnomah was one of the first steamboats to run on the Willamette River. (This boat should not be confused with the later, much better designed sternwheeler, Multnomah.) (Larry Barber Collection)

In May 1852, the *Multnomah* was sent to work on the lower Willamette River, running south from Canemah though the Willamette Valley. She also ran on the route from Portland on the Columbia River to the Cascades of the Columbia. The *Multnomah* was one of the fastest boats on the river. She could travel from Portland to Vancouver, Washington, in one hour and 20 minutes.

The *Multnomah* worked on Portland water routes to the Cascades until the fall of 1852 and was advertised as the "new and splendid steamer." She would run passengers between Oregon City and Portland, and connect there with the steamer *Lot Whitcomb*, which ran from Portland to Astoria. George Abernethy was *Multnomah*'s agent in Oregon City. Fares could be paid to him at his store or to the captain on board.

Using steamers for transportation was an economical way to get both people and freight around the area. The basic rates for steamboats in the early 1850s on the Oregon City-Portland run were $5 per passenger and $15 per ton of freight. (A ton was measured in volume, not weight; normally it equaled up to 100 cubic feet.)

In the early 1850s, rivalry was intense with the steamboats working on the lower Willamette River. To keep rates up, George S. Hoyt, owner of *Multnomah*, and Alexander S. Murray, owner of the sidewheeler *Portland*, formed the first steamboat company on the river. In 1853, the *Multnomah* was returned to the Portland - Oregon City route. Over her years of transport, some of her captains included John H. Couch, Richard Hoyt, Sr., H. L. Hoyt, John McNulty, William Molthrop, and W. H. Fauntleroy. The *Multnomah* was dismantled in Portland in 1864.

Marine propulsion became the new mechanism or system used to move a steamer across the water. Mixed paddle and propeller designs replaced the manual paddles, as they were more efficient and much easier to operate than the physical chore of moving a boat through the water. One of the first new apparatuses on a steamboat was the screw propeller driven engine invented in Scotland in the early 18th century. This new design was developed from the ordinary screw, from which the name originated. These primary propellers had only two blades and matched in shape the length of a single screw rotation. With screw propulsion, steam-driven equipment caused a shaft and a propeller fastened to it at the stern, to rotate. Force on the shaft tended at times to be extreme, and the boat required plenty of water in the days before tunnel-screw crafts adapted to shallow water navigation was developed. The screw propulsion mechanism tended to work best in a deep draft vessel traveling through salt water.

The propeller screw design was often found on steamboats by the 1880s, but inventors kept working with several other possibilities to make a variety of efficient blades. Soon the screw propeller driven boats had to step aside as another more powerful type of steamboat was emerging.

A paddlewheeler is steam operated, using paddlewheels to drive it through the water. There are two basic ways to inset paddle wheel wheels on a ship, either a single wheel on the rear, known as a sternwheeler, or a paddle wheel on each side, known as a sidewheeler. Today, diesel engines may power paddlewheels. This is the Sarah Dixon, a wooden sternwheel driven steamboat run by the Shaver Transportation Company on the Columbia River and the lower Willamette River, from 1892 to 1926.

(Shaver Transportation Collection)

The paddle wheel is a large waterwheel, where several scoops are set around the outside edge of the wheel. It is built on a steel framework, placed on the outer edge of the hull, and fitted with many paddle blades (called *floats* or *buckets*). About a quarter of the wheel travels underwater. Turning of the wheel makes a strong push through the water, either forward or backward as needed. (As more advanced paddle wheels were designed, they created a new feature, called *feathering*. A technique that kept each paddle blade positioned closer to vertical while it was in the water, which increased its speed.) The upper part of a paddle wheel is normally enclosed in a paddle box to decrease splashing.

The side paddlewheeler, or sidewheeler, enhanced the steam-driven propulsion with attached paddle wheels amidships to port and starboard rotating through the water. Under normal steaming operations, some of the buckets on the wheels would submerge as the wheels turned. When these wooden buckets were broken or lost by hitting river rocks, snags or other submerged entities, they could be simply replaced or repaired by docking the boat onto shore. Extra buckets were carried aboard.

The ability to make one wheel go around in a clockwise direction and the other counterclockwise was a useful feature of this means of drive. A sidewheeler had additional maneuverability since they are rigged so the paddles can move at various rates, and even in opposing directions. Because of their ability to move forward, reverse, and turn easily, the sidewheelers were favored for the harsh and narrow waters; they were commonly used on rivers and along the coastline. Sidewheelers are wider than a sternwheeler because of the extra width of the paddle wheels and their attached sponsons. Sponsons are protrusions from the sides of a vessel for stability and protection, or the fitting of gear or lifeboats. They extend a hull width on or below the waterline, help with keeping the craft afloat, and ease it through the waters. Sometimes, the overhangs were merely supported on brackets under the main deck or were plated over to protect them from the rivers and sea currents. The overhanging superstructure provided space for more passengers. This specialized build made the sidewheeler less efficient for daily routes. Unfortunately, both the sidewheeler and the screw propelled steamboats lacked the sternwheeler's ability to make an easy landing by nosing the prow up on the shore.

With the development of the sternwheeler, river traffic surged over the waters. In a simple modification from the sidewheeler, the sternwheeler had a rotated wheel affixed to the stern of the boat. As each bucket on the wheel in turn submerged, the vessel would be propelled forward or backward, depending on whether the wheel was in left to right or opposite motion. In addition, the boiler was commonly placed well forward on the hull in an effort to counterbalance the weight of the Pitman Rods and the sternwheel to distribute the primary weights evenly over the length of the hull. (A Pitman Rod is a connecting rod used to change from rotation to reciprocating motion.)

The sternwheeler was the most popular craft on the Columbia River as it did not require a deeper draft, such as propeller, and it didn't need docking facilities, which were very expensive to maintain. It turned swiftly in an extremely small area and could be handled easily in low water as well as through rapid water. Given the well-designed long shallow hull of a sternwheeler, it was able to carry extremely heavy cargoes. Successful maneuvering of a sternwheeler required that the draft of the hull at its stern did not vary much under all conditions of loading.

Wooden hulls were common because they could be repaired more economically and faster than iron hulls. Soft patches made out of wood were secured over holes, and even old beds might be tied over or stuffed into small holes until the steamer reached drydock for repairs. A sternwheeler with a wooden hull may well have lasted for five or six years without trouble, as long as it was maintained thoroughly, and actions were taken to prevent the hull from drying out, such as no icy conditions, and very few scrapes from the bottom. Whereas a steel hull provided more longevity, a wooden hull proved to be much more elastic. Unexpected encounters with gravel, boulders or a steep ditch, could cause a wooden hull to spring and splinter where a steel hull might develop a deep dent that would prove too costly to repair.

The wooden steam tugboat Jessie Harkins had been built by Jacob Kamm and named after L. P. (Lovelace Perne) Hosford's niece. The two men created the Harkins Transportation Company in 1914. (Shaver Transportation Collection)

Another wooden hulled sternwheeler, Elwood was built in Portland in 1891 for the Abernethy & Co. She carried both freight and passengers on the Willamette River under Captain J. L. Smith, followed by Captains R. Young and James Lee.

(Shaver Transportation Collection)

When the paddlewheeler became available in the Oregon Territory, the economy burst with trade, traffic and more settlers. These emerging qualities were very attractive to the Hudson's Bay Trading Company. With the wreck of two of their own sailing ships on the Pacific Coast, they brought the first sidewheeler to work on the Columbia River, the *S. S. Beaver* to Vancouver, B. C.

The Hudson's Bay Company had a sidewheeler steamship built on the banks of the Thames River in 1834 at Gravesend, England, costing about 2,500 pounds. She was designed for working on the west coast for their trading posts. The 187-ton *Beaver* was named in honor of the native northwest animal whose skins were much sought for by the Hudson Bay Company in the northwest.

The *Beaver* had a wooden hull made of English and African oak, elm, greenheart, and teak, and all fastenings were made of copper. She was double planked and had no figurehead; the only decoration she carried was the shield of the Hudson's Bay Company. She was 101 feet 4 inches long, with an 11-foot depth of hold, she drew a little over 8 feet, and the beam over her paddle boxes was 20 feet. She had 4 brass cannons and 63 ½ tons of machinery placed inside her hold before the decks were laid.

The *Beaver* had two 35-horsepower side lever steam engines each with cylinders of 35 ½ inches in diameter and a stroke of 36 inches. (A steam engine is a heat engine that performs mechanical work using steam as its working solution. The horsepower depended primarily upon the size of the pistons and steam-pressure developed.) These powerful engines turned the shaft for her side wheels, each of which was 13 feet in diameter with buckets 6 ½ feet long and mounted well forward. It was rather a simple arrangement. The *Beaver* had a rectangular boiler that could burn either wood or coal and generated steam-pressure at under 3 psi (pounds per square inch). The steam was then injected to give the pressure that pushed the horizontal pistons that moved the pitmans that turned the big paddle wheels and was fed by seawater. Below the boilers were brick furnaces which when well stoked could create enough steam to turn the wheels 30 times a minute and send the ship through the water at about 9 miles per hour.

Since her Boulton and Watt engines were not pressure engines, but were vacuum engines, they could use salt water at low-pressure. The salt water destroyed the boilers as the salinity rusted the wall thickness, eventually rotting them out. The *Beaver* had to have a new boiler every seven years or so and went through several installations over her term of service. Over time the boiler pressure was worn down, and the large 42 inch cylinders were replaced with 36 inch diameter ones. Her biggest advantage was that the steamboat could run with either sails or steam.

The *Beaver* was launched at the shipyard Blackwell Yard near London, May 7, 1835, with 150,000 admirers watching, including King William of England. She then left her homeport, rigged with sails on August 29, 1835, for her 163-day voyage to the west coast of North America. This sidewheeler was outfitted as a brig (a two-masted, square-rigged vessel with an extra gaff sail on the mainmast) for the passage from London. The *Beaver* came out via Cape Horn, South America, only on sail under the command of Captain David Home, a 12-man crew including the mate, W. C. Hamilton, second mate Charles Dodd, chief engineer Peter Arthur, and second engineer John Donald. Traveling with them was the company's three mast sailing ship, the *Columbia*. Despite the *Beaver* having just the power of a steamship, she proved to be more seaworthy, and she had to slow her pace so as not to lose her seafaring companion. On September 30, as the vessels neared the equator, Captain Home lost sight of the *Columbia*. It wasn't until after steaming through risky storms did the captain spot her. They met at Juan Fernandez Island off the coast of Chile. From there, they both sailed for Hawaii, arriving on February 4, 1836. She stayed in Honolulu for three weeks to overhaul and restock supplies before starting on the final passage to Washington.

The vessels arrived off the Columbia River on March 18, 1836, and anchored off Fort Vancouver on April 10. Once she settled, the previously shipped paddlewheels, boilers, and engines were assembled on the lower decks. In the afternoon of May 17, the *Beaver* made her first trial run under steam power, towing the *Columbia* a short distance down the river. The crew used her coal supply quickly as she burned about one ton of coal every hour. To continue the voyage up the Columbia River, the heavy little boat's boilers consumed a supply of 40 cords of wood, which took six men two days to cut. It burned through this supply between just 12 and 14 hours while steaming 230 miles to maintain a speed of 6 knots (A knot is 1 nautical mile per hour). A long excursion required about as much time tied up along the shore so the crew could gather wood as the boat actually spent on the water. A few days later, the *Beaver* traveled around Sauvie Island.

Steamboats burned an average of four cords of wood an hour. Their powerful boilers offered steady jobs for hundreds of woodcutters. Many vessels, propelled by either sail or steam, hauled cordwood from timber mills set along the riverside to power boats, and then carried more trees to be dropped down for fuel. The cycle went from such timber scarce upriver landings as The Dalles, to logging mills west of the Cascades. Much of Portland's Irvington district, once thick woodland, was cut over to provide steamboat fuel.

Ironically, on July 17 of that same year, the *Beaver* left on its first voyage from Fort Vancouver and it never returned to the Columbia River. Dr. John McLoughlin didn't like the boat and had fought with the plans to build it from the start. He thought it unnecessary, as there were no trading stations between Astoria and Fort Vancouver, and he was concerned that it drew too much water at eight feet for the rapidly changing river. He dispatched the ship to the company's Nisqually trading post at the southern end of Puget Sound.

The *Beaver* became a floating trading post that opened up remote parts of the waters in locations as far away as the Russian settlement in Sitka and the British Columbia coast for fur trading. By the 1840s, wood was seldom burned as fuel for steamships, so she was then sent for transporting coal along the coastline. While the *Beaver* burned coal, the company would hire young natives of the Squamish Nation to work the holds as coal passers.

Later, the *Beaver* helped the Hudson's Bay Company establish Fort Victoria in 1843 and in the creating of coal mines at Fort Rupert in Nanaimo, on Vancouver Island in 1853. Fort Rupert was a Hudson's Bay Company fort, located near present day Port Hardy, British Columbia, on Vancouver Island.

After nearly 15 years, the *Beaver* was alone in her glory as the only steamer in the waters of the western world. She formed an important connection for the Hudson's Bay Company, ranging over routes from San Francisco on the south to Sitka on the north, distributing supplies for the large fur company and picking up furs in return. The Hudson's Bay Company brought in the wooden sidewheeler the *Otter,* which became the second steamship to work in the Pacific Northwest. Almost identical to the *Beaver*, but she had a more powerful propeller, the *Otter* was used to help the trading posts between Puget Sound and Alaska.

The Hudson's Bay Company sent the *Beaver* to carry passengers and cargo up north for a few more years. Under the command of Lt. Daniel Pender of the Royal Navy, the *Beaver* was commissioned from 1863 to 1870, to be used as a survey vessel. She could edge her way into isolated bays where her crew surveyed and charted 1,000 miles of coastline of the British Columbia coast.

The *Beaver* worked in the Hudson's Bay Company for 40 years. The sturdy little ship had a symbolic value for the company. In 1874, a conglomerate that became the British Columbia Towing and Transportation Company purchased the *Beaver*. She was used as a towboat and towed barges, log booms and sailing vessels until July 25, 1888, when, due to strong currents and Captain George Marchant's navigational error, she went aground on rocks at Prospect Point in Stanly Park, Vancouver, B. C. No one was killed or seriously injured. She finally sank in July of 1892 from the wake of the passing steamer *Yosemite.* Her planners had built well, half a century before, and she outlasted her contemporaries, including her larger consort *Columbia*, and many later, more modern boats as well.

Many steamboats were called the Beaver. The one shown here was originally named the G. W. Shaver, then later the Glenola. This Beaver had been rebuilt in Portland in 1906, extending her length to 152 feet with a 30-foot beam and 6-foot hold.

(Shaver Transportation Collection)

Even though The Dalles remained the center of early river traffic, it was spreading west each day. By the late 1840s and early 1850s, oceangoing ships equipped with supporting steam engines traveled from The Dalles up the lower river as far as Portland, Oregon, and Fort Vancouver, Washington. Slightly over a decade later, commercial steamboats began regular service on the Columbia River. Because of the increase in maritime transportation, the passenger trade on the lower Columbia, as well as above the Cascades, had become of value, otherwise, it could not have supported so many steamboats.

In 1881, the freight and steam sternwheeler Washington was built in Vancouver, Washington. She measured at 292.28 gross tons and 193.09 feet in length. Here she is on the Columbia River. (Oregon Maritime Museum Collection)

Abernethy & Company brought out other steamships to work around Canemah. For example, three steamboats were loaded on the ship *Success* from New York, along with its regular delivery of merchandise. Two of the steamers that arrived were small iron propellers. The third, *Multnomah*, was a wooden sidewheeler.

The reality of building steamboats right here in Oregon rather than paying for the shipment of boats and their attachments soon became the norm in the Northwest. The *Washington* and the *Allen* were both iron hulled and driven by propellers. These steamers started a daily service between Portland and Oregon City and towed in their spare time. Many sternwheelers were being built and operating along both the Columbia and Willamette Rivers.

In 1851, D. F. Bradford and Captain Van Bergen were determined to bring growth to the middle stretch of the Columbia River. They brought in an engine and put together a hull that would become an 80-foot long sidewheeler with a 12-foot beam, the *James P. Flint.*

She ran a few trips back and forth from the Cascades to The Dalles, carrying migrants and their accessories and livestock on the down trips and a few army troops and supplies on the upriver runs. Once the seasonal needs were met, commerce disappeared.

The steamer Altona is on the Willamette River in Oregon City waiting to take passengers to Portland. (Larry Barber Collection)

Both Bradford and Van Bergen realized that their boat was stationed too far from the town, so they decided take it to the businesses. To do that, they had to haul her up on the bank, put skids under her, and drag her around the worst of the rapids until they could find stable water again. Once below the Cascades, the *James P. Flint* went back to work in 1852. In September, she smashed against a rock near Cape Horn, Washington, on the riverbank and sank, leaving her upper works above the water.

With the destruction of the *James P. Flint,* a new template emerged. In January of 1853, she was pumped out, patched, and taken to Vancouver where each piece was repaired and restored. Her hull and cabin were still very useable, but her engine wasn't any good. Her valuable parts were later used in a new steamer.

In 1860, steamboat operators joined forces to capitalize on the growing industry in transporting goods and people on the Columbia. The new company was formed by John C. Ainsworth and Simeon Reed of Portland, and Robert R. Thompson, originally of The Dalles. They named their business the Oregon Steam Navigation Company (OSNC). It would monopolize river transportation for the next 20 years.

During that time, while the OSNC ran many vessels on the Columbia River, the Oregon Steamship Company offered passenger service on coastal steamships from San Francisco, California, to Portland, Oregon.

The Oregon Railroad and Navigation Company (ORNC), founded in 1879, ran a rail network of 1,143 miles of track from Portland to northeastern Oregon, northwestern Oregon and Washington, and northern Idaho. The railroad company wanted to take over the waters as well as the railroads, so they purchased the Oregon Steam Navigation Company in 1880, and gave it a gave it a limited route on the Oregon side of the Columbia River. The ORNC then sought after an expansion of its Columbia River route, surveying from where the Oregon Steam Navigation tracks ended at Celilo and continuing east to Wallula, Washington. Their only active competition began in 1880, with the new business, the Shaver Transportation Company located in Portland, Oregon.

By 1882, the ORNC bought the Oregon Steamship Company and their course along the Columbia River was complete. They now owned the large steamships, *Columbia, City of Chester, George W. Elder, Olympian,* and *Oregon.*

The Union Pacific Railroad bought a majority stake of the ORNC in 1898. Their fleet listing from June 30, 1898, to June 30, 1899, included *T. J. Potter, R. R. Thompson, Harvest Queen,* and both the original *Hassalo,* and the one built in 1898-99. In 1936, Union Pacific Railroad formally absorbed the ORNC, which became the Union Pacific Railroad's access to the entire Pacific Northwest.

ONE MAN, MANY STERNWHEELERS

No other person had a longer career in the steamboat business in the Pacific Northwest than James D. Miller. Over his career, Miller commanded 36 steamboats, on the Tualatin, Willamette, Columbia, and Kootenay Rivers. Miller was a steamboat captain from 1851 to 1903. He became well known for his long time of service with the large number of liners he controlled, and the many geographical areas in which he served.

Captain Miller was born on the east coast of America in 1830. He came out to the Pacific Coast in 1848. Arriving in Oregon, Miller traded his horses and mules for an acre of land in a place called Clackamas City, just north of Oregon City.

In the spring of 1850, Miller built a flatboat 65 feet long, which could haul 350 bushels of wheat. He ran his boat between Canemah barely above the Willamette Falls and Dayton, on the Yamhill River. He hired four native Americans of the Klickitat First Nation as crew; they poled and rowed the boat up the Yamhill River to Dayton and Lafayette. It took two days to go up from Canemah, and one day to return downriver. Miller charged $35 a ton to haul cargo upriver to farmers, which were often consignments from merchants on the lower Willamette River. Coming down the river, Miller charged 50 cents a bushel to carry out the farmers' wheat. His main expenses were the salaries of his First Nation crew, which were $16 per man for each trip.

Miller stayed in the flatboat business for about a year when on May 19, 1851, the first steamboat appeared on the Upper Willamette. This was a small sidewheeler only 50 feet in length, the *Hoosier*. Although very basic, the *Hoosier* could haul much more cargo and wheat than any flatboat, up to 5 tons, so Miller was soon out of business. After meeting with John Zumwalt, the owner, he did manage a new job. Miller worked as the bookkeeper, purser, pilot, and deckhand.

In the fall of 1856 with his brother-in-law Silas R. Smith, Miller bought the *Hoosier*. Within the next year, they built another steamboat in Canemah, a sidewheeler, the *Hoosier No. 2*. Miller worked the steamer on the Willamette between Champoeg and Butteville up the Yamhill River. In 1857, he reconstructed *Hoosier No. 2* raising her weight up to 27 tons and called her the *Hoosier No. 3*.

In 1858, Miller sold his interest in *Hoosier No. 3* to E.M. White. With some partners, he purchased the sternwheeler *James Clinton*, and ran her until April 23, 1861. A dockside fire in Linn City, near Canemah, destroyed the *Clinton*. Two years later, he took the machinery out of *Hoosier* and placed it in the steam scow, *Yamhill*.

On December 1, 1861, when the Great Flood of 1862 or Noachian Deluge, the largest flood in the recorded history of Oregon, Nevada, and California hit the Willamette River, Miller's home was thought to be the safest building in the town and other people sheltered there during the storm. As the water rose, it became clear that they would have to evacuate his home, which they did just before the building was swept away. Miller's home was demolished, along with most of Linn City.

Except for a short time in 1862, when he was on the steamers, *Mountain Buck* and *Julia Barclay*, Miller ran the sternwheeler *Union* on the Willamette River until 1866 when the People's Transportation Company acquired the vessel. (The People's Transportation Company, an organization under the general incorporation law of Oregon, entered the scene in 1862. This company built the canal, basin, and warehouse on the east side of the Willamette River. They put the *E. D. Baker*, a sternwheeler, on the lower Columbia, the *Iris*, a sidewheeler, on the middle, and the *Kiyus*, a sternwheeler, on the upper Cascades. They carried on a profitable trade between Portland and the various points upriver, until finally selling out to Ben Holladay, who, with his railroad and river steamboats, then held command of the trade of the entire Willamette Valley.) From the sternwheeler *Union*, Miller went as pilot on the *Fanny Patton* with Captain George Jerome. After that, Miller moved to the sternwheeler *Enterprise* (built in 1863) with Captain Sebastian "Bas" Miller; he stayed there until that boat was demolished.

In 1886, Miller piloted the new steamer sternwheeler *Albany* with Captain Lon Vickers. (This boat should not be confused with the later sternwheeler with the same name. The *N. S. Bentley* was rebuilt and called the *Albany*. She also ran on the Willamette River from 1896 to 1906. She was then rebuilt again, and called the *Georgie Burton*.) After a brief stay on the *Albany*, Miller joined the lumber commerce in Oregon City. Later, he served on the People's Transportation Company's steamers *Onward*, *Senator*, and the *E. N. Cooke*. Miller was a passenger on the 132-foot sternwheeler *Senator* when she blew up on May 6, 1875, at the foot of Alder Street dock in Portland. A terrific explosion blew the pilothouse 100 feet into the air and wrecked the forward portion of the steamer. Captain Dan McGill at the wheel, five crew members, and one passenger were killed outright and seven others were injured. Twenty passengers survived without serious injuries. A coroner's jury ruled "insufficient water in the boiler." The engineer was arrested on a charge of manslaughter but was later acquitted.

The next day, Miller took command of the *E. N. Cooke*, and ran her until the Oregon Steam Navigation Company took in the People's Transportation Company. In 1878, Miller invested in a number of flour mills and bought the 148-foot sternwheeler *A. A. McCully*. Miller removed the geared machinery from the steamer and installed it in the sternwheeler *Success*. Miller took the *Success* up the Willamette River to Eugene, Oregon. In 1879, Miller suffered some financial difficulties, losing not only his mill interest but the steamer as well. Miller then took command of the sternwheeler *City of Salem*, and ran her until 1881 for William Reid's business, the Oregon Railway. Miller carried railroad cargo to Ray's Landing and Dayton.

Because of his poor health, Miller resigned from the command of the *City of Salem*, and with others bought the flour mills in Walla Walla, Washington Territory. He left the mills to his partners to run, went to Sand Point, Idaho, and ran the *Henry Villard* on Lake Pend Oreille. After this steamer, he worked on the *Katie Hallet*, running it on the Clarks Fork Yellowstone River.

In the spring of 1882 Miller returned to Walla Walla, sold out his share of the mills and went back to Dayton, Oregon. By 1889, he returned to the waters and began piloting the *City of Salem* again. He worked on this steamer, running it between Fulquartz Landing and Ray's Landing, Oregon until 1890.

Miller then decided to go to Huntington, Oregon. He was still intrigued with the building of these fine boats, so he oversaw the building of the sternwheeler *Norma* with Jacob Kamm in 1891. She made her first trip with Miller on board into the Seven Devils country. This was a 60-mile run downriver into Hells Canyon, Oregon, to Seven Devils Landing, and then back upriver to Huntington. After this achievement, Miller returned to Portland and served on the sternwheelers *Gov. Newell*, *Three Sisters*, *Toledo*, and *Joseph Kellogg* from 1891 to 1892.

In 1893, Miller went to Montana and took command of the steamer *Annerly*, running on the upper Kootenay (also Kootenai) River between Jennings, Montana, and Fort Steele, B. C. He remained there until August of 1894, when he went to Puget Sound to buy the steamer *Halys*, and had her shipped inland to be placed on the lower Kootenay River, running out of Bonner's Ferry, Idaho. Miller ran steamboats in the Kootenai, Idaho, region until 1901. During 1902 to 1903, Miller commanded steamboats on the reach of the Columbia River above the Wenatchee, Washington. In addition to the boats already mentioned, he worked on the *Elwood*, *Multnomah*, *Undine*, and *Chelan*.

Captain Miller died in 1914 in Oregon. James D. Miller, Captain Miller's son, was also a steamboat pilot.

Captain W. P. Gray overloaded the Norma with staging lumber to ward off the blows of sharp rocks. Gray navigated down the Snake River. He wrecked her along the mouth of the Deschutes River. (Oregon Maritime Museum Collection)

Another active steamer, *Columbia* was built in 1850 in Upper Astoria. She was the first steamboat constructed in Oregon. The *Columbia* was a small ferry type of sidewheeler, 90 feet long, 16-foot beam, about 4-foot of depth of hold, and 75 tons burden. It is believed that General James Adair and James Frost built her. (Other records state that George Hewitt, Thomas Goodwin, Frost, and others made her. Part of this confusion is that this craft has the same name as many other boats called *Columbia*. At least four other vessels were named *Columbia* and ran on the Columbia River and its tributaries, such as the propeller-driven excursion steamer *Columbia* built in 1904. Frank Kirby, one of the leading naval architects of the time, designed that one.) This *Columbia* was given her name because she was the first craft to enter the Columbia River.

The *Columbia* was built for General John Adair, Captain Daniel Frost and the firm of Leonard & Green, located in Upper Astoria. Even though the *Columbia* was a small sidewheeler, she cost over $25,000 to build as the mechanics were paid at the rate of sixteen dollars per day, and other workers received five to eight dollars in gold.

This sidewheeler was unusual and awkward in appearance. She was double ended like a ferryboat, built entirely of wood, and powered by sidewheels which were driven by the latest designed engines of that time. These special engines had been ordered from France. One designer had traveled to San Francisco to pick up delivery of the engines and have them then shipped up to Astoria.

With Captain Frost in command, she made her trial trip on July 3, 1850, from Astoria to Portland and Oregon City. She traveled towards the Columbia River channel through rough waters, heading away from the Pacific Ocean. After her first day on the water, she had gone fifty miles. Captain Frost did not want to run the *Columbia* at night, so he berthed her along the riverbank. The next morning, the captain headed her upstream towards Portland. She reached Portland at 3:00 p.m. the next day. Because the river was new to him, Captain Frost took his time easing her through the narrow channel. It took nearly 2 days just to get to Portland. On his last stop in Oregon City, there was a great festivity for her arrival.

The *Columbia* was the first steamer to set up regular service on the lower Willamette and Columbia Rivers. She could hold up to twenty passengers. (Steamboat capacity was measured by tonnage. The total volume capacity of the vessel was measured in gross tonnage. Registered tonnage was the total "speculative" volume that could be used to carry cargo or passengers when the mechanical, fuel, and comparable quarters had been removed from its weight.)

Once the *Columbia*'s schedule had been refined, she made the Oregon City - Portland - Astoria and Vancouver run twice a month at 4 miles per hour, charging $25 per passenger, and $25 per ton of freight, under the command of Captain Frost.

The *Columbia* was a simple boat, without luxuries of any kind, not even a passenger cabin or a galley. Since the *Columbia* docked in Upper Astoria, all freight and passengers had to come on board in that part of town. Passengers brought their own blankets and lunch baskets. During the evenings, free deck space was assigned for sleeping.

The *Columbia* would leave Astoria at noon after connecting with an ocean ship that came up north from San Francisco owned by the Pacific Mail Steamship Company. Taking their passengers and cargo, she would then arrive in Portland at 3 p.m. the next day. After waiting there for a few hours, she continued to Oregon City, reaching there by 8 in the evening. Since she was tied up at night, her travel time between Astoria and Portland was twenty-four hours.

Another way this sidewheeler made money was that she carried cargo and supplies from Vancouver to the Cascades; sometimes she took passengers from the Pacific Mail steamers in Astoria as well. Sometimes there were so many on board, it was standing room only. The *Columbia* ran for a year or two, until more efficient and quicker boats were brought in, taking her trade.

In January of 1853, the *Columbia*'s machinery, including her solid engine, were taken out and put into a new sidewheeler, called the *Fashion*. Part of this new boat also had the hull and cabin from the *James P. Flint*. The *Fashion* ran the Cowlitz River to the Cascades until 1861, commanded by Capt. J.O. Van Bergen. The sidewheeler covered many routes, going to the Cowlitz Monday and Tuesday, Oregon City Wednesday and Thursday, and the rest of the week to Vancouver and the Cascades.

Until December of 1850, the *Columbia* held a monopoly on the northwest rivers. That winter, the sidewheeler *Lot Whitcomb* was built just down a ways in one of the most lively and promising towns in Oregon: Milwaukie. She was the first steamboat ever built on the Willamette River. Mr. Lot Whitcomb, a successful industrialist, had no experience with piloting a steamboat, but he had diligence, so he went out and recruited a team of investors and builders. Lot Whitcomb, Colonel Jennings, S. S. White, and others spent about $80,000 on labor and material. They modeled the *Lot Whitcomb* after the style of a Hudson River steamboat, using a mixture of Mississippi and East Coast designs.

She was a fine boat, being both strong and fast. The *Lot Whitcomb* was much larger than the *Columbia*: 160 feet long and built from a solid pole of Oregon fir. She had a 24-foot beam, over 5 feet of draft, and 600 gross tons. Her sidewheels were 18 feet in diameter. Her keel was 12x14 inches, and she had a 17-inch cylinder with a 7-foot stroke. Her steam engine of 140 horsepower was constructed by Jacob Kamm in New Orleans and then shipped in pieces to Oregon.

She had twin boilers set forward and on the guards were raised tall stacks. Her sidewheels were in housings that rose above the Texas deck and were set well back from center. (The Texas is the topmost deckhouse on the typical steamer.) She had a closed boiler deck, a long cabin deck, and a simple pilothouse, which were located nearly in the middle, behind the chimneys. Her burden was 600 tons, but she proved to be a safe and efficient boat. When loaded, she would draw about three feet, and she would make twelve miles an hour on the Columbia River.

The *Lot Whitcomb* was much more comfortable than her predecessor was, and her looks were very impressive. All of her upper works were painted white, without decoration; on each wheel housing was her name in simple letters. Her cabins were carefully decorated and done in the best cabinetwork and paneling. She had plenty of cabinet space, a ladies' cabin, and a dining hall.

One of the very first river pilots on the *Columbia* became the captain of the *Lot Whitcomb*. John C. Ainsworth was from Iowa, where he had been involved in

30

steamboating on the Mississippi between St. Louis and Galena for about five years. Barely 28 years old when he came to Oregon in 1850, Ainsworth was eager to make a name for himself as a maritime hand.

The *Lot Whitcomb* was launched from the banks of the Willamette River on Christmas day, 1850. That was a great day in Oregon; hundreds from all parts of the country came to witness the new steamboat. By act of the Territorial Legislature, she would be named the *Lot Whitcomb of Oregon*. Governor Gaines came to Oregon City to make it official and gave a speech to send her on her way. The *Lot Whitcomb* then slid sideways off the cradle and into the water. Mayor Kilborn bestowed a set of colors to her, and he too gave a praising address to the creators of this first-rate sidewheeler. Once the ceremonials were finished, the merriment began. As expected, cannons had to be fired, and for some unknown reason, the salute cannon blew up, killing a participant. Otherwise, it was a very joyful event, and the whole affair ended in a grand ball, the music provided by the Oregon City brass band. The festivities were kept up for three days and nights.

With the *Lot Whitcomb* willing to offer a stiff rivalry, in January of 1851, the master of the *Columbia* reduced her fare to $15 between Portland and Astoria. The *Lot Whitcomb* refused to match this rate, knowing that the advantages of grace and speed were in her favor. Instead, she offered a more attractive schedule: she would leave Milwaukie on Mondays and Thursdays at noon, stopping at Portland, Fort Vancouver, St. Helens, Cowlitz, and Cathlamet on her way to Astoria. When the water was favorable, she would return from Pacific City to Oregon City. She charged only $20 for this trip between Milwaukie, Portland, or Fort Vancouver to Astoria, $2 between Milwaukie and Portland, and $5 between Milwaukie and Vancouver. There was an added fee of $2 to go down to Oregon City from Milwaukie; board was not included in these rates.

The *Lot Whitcomb* took most of the *Columbia*'s business. Captain Ainsworth could run her upriver 120 miles from Astoria to Oregon City in ten hours, where it took the *Columbia* two days. He got her down to less than an hour run from Milwaukie down to Oregon City.

The Portland merchants resented the aggressive service of the *Lot Whitcomb*. They worked together, purchased a 172-foot ocean steamship, the *Goldwater*, and put her into service running between Portland and San Francisco, including coastal ports, such as Astoria. This caused a big benefit for Portland, which quickly overtook Milwaukie and Oregon City in size, forcing the *Whitcomb* to transfer to Portland.

The *Lot Whitcomb* continued to work on the lower river routes until August of 1854, but she was getting too expensive to use. She was then sold to a California firm for use on the Sacramento River. The steamship *Peytonia* towed her down to San Francisco. Captain Ainsworth went along on the trip, which faced very stormy weather conditions. By the time they reached San Francisco, the *Lot Whitcomb* had three feet of water in her hold. Once she arrived and was pumped out, the California Steam Navigation Company took over, and renamed her *Annie Abernathy*. There, she ran the Napa Creek and Sacramento routes for the California Steam Navigation Company until 1868.

(Oregon Maritime Museum Collection)

"The launch of the Lot Whitcomb, a steamer built in Milwaukie on Christmas Day, 1850, opened a century of transporting goods and passengers by water on the upper and lower Willamette River."

-Karin Morey, Clackamas County Historical Society Manager

The need for an efficient mail service was desired in Oregon and the steamers seemed to be the best transport. The Pacific Mail Steamship Company, a New York corporation that had the mail contract between Panama and Oregon, brought out a large iron hulled propeller called the *Willamette*. She was built for the Pacific Mail Steamship Company at Wilmington, Delaware, and brought around Cape Horn, South America, under sail as a three-masted schooner, arriving in the fall of 1851.

The *Willamette* was intended only for shuttle service between Astoria and Oregon City; the *Willamette* arrived on the Columbia River under schooner rig, with her engines disconnected. While trailing the *Lot Whitcomb* at the end of a hawser, she was taken to Portland for fitting and quickly put to service. By July she was doing her job, meeting the bi-monthly steamer in Astoria and bringing its passengers, mail and freight upriver.

She worked under Captain Durbrow, between Portland and Astoria in connection with the Company's sea steamer. She was a stylish boat including excellent accommodations for passengers, and great freight capacity. Because she was built too large for the trade, in August of 1852, her owners took her to California and ran her on the Sacramento River.

In 1851, the propeller powered *Eagle* with an iron hull was assembled at the higher end of the Cascade Rapids and put into service between the Cascades and The Dalles. The steamer *Eagle* wasn't any larger than an ordinary ship's yawl boat, only about 40 feet long, with room for nearly a dozen passengers, or 20 tons of freight.

Captains William Wells and Richard Williams owned the *Eagle* and ran her from Vancouver to Portland then to Oregon City. While Wells ran the ship, Williams was mate, fireman, and "all hands", and when Williams took the wheel, Wells became the crew. She would leave Vancouver at half past eight in the morning and arrive in Portland by noon. She carried freight for $15 per ton and $5 for each passenger - good pay for a twelve mile route. When needed, she would go to Oregon City, otherwise, she'd start back for Vancouver at 3 p.m. and tie up at home by six in the evening. The *Eagle* made more money given her size than any other boat in Oregon. She ran for 20 years, carrying the longest working life of these early steamers. Out of her earnings, the captains built the iron steamboat *Belle* and made themselves chief owners in the *Senorita-two*, both of which were first class steamboats.

There was also a propeller boat, the *Hoosier*, working on the same waters as the *Eagle*; she was a reconstruction of a ship's longboat with engines of the pinion gear type with both the engine and boiler coming out of a former pile. She could be heard splashing along the Willamette with her grinding pile driven engine.

Although small and rudimentary, the *Hoosier* was the first of many steamboats to work the shallow waters of the 11-mile long Yamhill River (a tributary of the Willamette River). She could also haul much more cargo and wheat than any flatboat. John Zumwalt, her owner, hired Captain James Miller to run his steamer as the bookkeeper, purser, and pilot. The *Hoosier* worked Portland, and then was moved up around the falls in Oregon City where she became the first steamboat to work on the Upper Willamette. In June of 1851, the *Hoosier* was making many trips a week from Canemah (the landing a mile above the falls) to Dayton on the Yamhill River. Soon after her success, over thirty other steamboats were built in Canemah in just three months.

Captain Miller bought the *Hoosier* in the fall of 1856 and the following year built the first sidewheeler steamship, *Hoosier* (named after the propeller boat). Much like her predecessor, this *Hoosier* could be heard from a great distance, her rods clattering, and her gears screeching. Usually the first sign of a coming steamboat was a cloud of smoke beyond a bend and a faint sound from her whistle followed by the rhythmic spurts of the escape pipes and wheel - but the new *Hoosier* carried a mechanical sound along the waters.

Captain Miller ran this vessel on the Willamette between Champoeg and Butteville and up the Yamhill River. He later built the third *Hoosier* and sold an interest to investor E. M. White. Captain Miller bought the 90-foot sternwheeler *James Clinton* and worked her until April 23, 1861. She was the first boat to go as far as Eugene. A dockside fire in Linn City, Oregon, wrecked the Clinton. In 1860, Captain Miller took all the machinery out of the *Clinton* and placed it in the steam scow *Yam.*

In September of 1851, three months after the *Hoosier* had begun working the upper river, another prominent steamer appeared on the waters. The *Canemah* was a light draft 135-foot, 48-ton wooden sidewheeler manufactured back east and shipped out to Oregon, then assembled in the town for which it was named. The *Canemah* was large and was the first steamer to enter a regularly scheduled service. She worked on both the Willamette and Yamhill Rivers as far up as Dayton.

She was built and launched by Captain Absalom F. Hedges, who arrived by covered wagon in 1844; he had been a carpenter and steamboat captain on the Ohio River. In 1849, he platted Falls City and headed to New York to buy steamboat machinery. Once he staked his donation land claim, he founded the town of Canemah. (The name of this town is from the Chinook tribe for "the canoe place," a description of the sandy beach and inland harbor that brought thousands of native Americans here during annual salmon runs.)

Captain Hedges and his partners, Captain Charles Bennett, Alanson Beers, Hamilton Campbell, and John McClosky, all recognized that this area was a natural place to develop a shipbuilding center. The *Canemah* was their first prodigy. Her first commanders were captains Charles Bennett (killed by native

34

Americans in 1855) and John McClosky. In October of 1851, the *Canemah* made its first trip up the Willamette River as far as Corvallis.

By 1852, the *Canemah* showed to be a profitable steamer; she got the contract for becoming a floating post office for Nathaniel Coe, the postal agent for the Oregon Territory. Coe sorted all the letters and parcels as the *Canemah* traveled along the river, picking up and dropping off the post at each landing. She made the mail route twice a week between the towns of Canemah and Salem. Each time she docked, it meant the arrival of produce and travelers, which was an occasion of great excitement for people waiting along the shore.

Mail distribution was very different then; sometimes it occurred when people would wave a letter at a landing just to flag the steamer down. Mail was carried upriver, and the boat earned 20 cents a bushel hauling grain downriver from places like the Avery Brothers warehouse in Corvallis to Canemah. For example, the *Canemah* could load 1,000 to 1,500 packets a voyage. (The heaviest load she ever carried was 35 tons.) For several years after that, the *Canemah* made weekly trips between Oregon City and Marysville. Because of the increase of steamboats, there was a steamboat landing built at both Upper Marysville and Lower Marysville.

The *Canemah* had all the problems other steamboats had, but her greatest was fuel. Though she drew only 17 inches loaded and could run anywhere it was damp, she had to stay near the bank if she was running low on cordwood for the furnaces. The crew paid five dollars a cord, but during the first years of steamboating, only a few wood yards were found. With any luck, a steamer might start on a run, and hope to find a farmer willing to sell wood. If it did, the captain haggled, and the crew loaded, if it did not, the boat would have to turn back, using its steam as sparingly as possible, while taking advantage of the current. When the loads were small, a boat could start a run with enough wood aboard to last the trip.

As many more vessels were being built and used along the rivers, many problems arose with each ship. Unfortunately, the *Canemah* became the first steamboat explosion in Oregon. On August 8, 1853, near the Champoeg landing on the Willamette River, her flued boiler detonated. (A flued or shell boiler was an early and relatively simple type of boiler used for making steam, typically to drive a steam engine.) While the steamship survived, her explosion was big enough to scald a passenger, Marion Holcroft, to death.

In 1854, the *Canemah* was sold to the Citizens Accommodation Line, a company owned by Captains Hedges and George E. Cole, and E.M. White. The partnership dissolved when the native Americans in Colonel Kelly's fight on the Touchet killed Captain Hedges in 1856, but the Citizen Accommodation Line kept expanding. Soon Cole and White bought the sidewheeler *Franklin* and worked both vessels from the town of Canemah. They now had a carriage line that hauled passengers up from Oregon City along the one or two miles of road to where twice a week the *Canemah* or *Franklin* departed for Corvallis. The *Franklin*, 93 feet in length and 49 gross tons, also ran three times a week carrying local cargo to Salem. Meals were a dollar each and some companies included beds.

Most of the rates were standard. Freight went from Portland to Oregon City for $3 a ton, from Canemah to Champoeg was $10, $16 to Salem, $20 to Albany, and $14 to Corvallis. Beyond these stops, the carrier was left to barter with flatboat men and ox-driven freight coaches all on his own. By 1858, with more advanced steamers on the water, the *Canemah* was dismantled.

THE LIFE OF A SIDEWHEELER: THE *GAZELLE*

In the summer of 1853, a company of California entrepreneurs bought the land on the west side of the Willamette Falls, near where the canal locks are situated today. They built a basin and warehouse. Their first boat was burned on the stocks October 6, 1853, but their second was the ill-fated *Gazelle*, a large and stunning sidewheeler. She was one of the first to work on the Willamette River, but she did not last long, her double engine boilers exploded and destroyed her. (Boiler explosions were frequent with the early sternwheelers. Firing the boiler to increase the steam-pressure beyond adequate limits is commonly believed to be the main cause of these explosions, or the steamer could have been running with insufficient reserve water in the boiler system. Running light on water makes for a speedy steaming, but if the water in the boiler falls below a standard level, the boilerplates could become red hot and explode. Another theory for this common incident was the defects in the steel strength or the breakdown of the safety valves due to corrosion, caused by dirty river feed water.)

The *Gazelle* was built on the west side of the Willamette River, in Canemah, just across from Oregon City. She was 145 feet in length and was driven by two steam engines, each one turning one of her sidewheels. *Gazelle*'s builders were doing business as the Willamette Falls Canal, Milling, and Transportation Company. The plan was to have her work on the Willamette River above the falls, to offer services for the growing population in the Willamette Valley. To reach the upper river, the *Gazelle* was lifted above the falls and launched on the upper Willamette at Canemah.

The *Gazelle* made her trial run above the Willamette Falls on March 18, 1854, with her first captain Robert Hereford. During the voyage, the *Gazelle* stood by as the new sidewheeler *Oregon* was sinking in 8 feet of water after hitting a snag just below the town of Salem. Cargo from the *Oregon* was loaded onto *Gazelle* to lighten her and allow her easier salvaging. Suddenly the *Oregon* broke free of the snag, drifted downstream, ran up on a sandbar and sank so deeply that only a part of her upper works were visible above the water; she was a total loss. On the way back down, the *Gazelle* ran over a log and broke some paddle buckets, which was not serious damage, and in fact was one of the strengths of the paddlewheel design over the propeller on inland waters.

At 6:30 a.m. on April 8, 1858, the *Gazelle* had come over to Canemah from the long wharf built above the Willamette Falls on the western side of the river above Linn City. This was to be her first regular run after the trip upriver where she'd attempted to aid the *Oregon*. That morning, she was headed for Corvallis. The *Gazelle* had been at the Canemah dock for about ten minutes, but to make a speedy departure, the engineer had tied down the safety valve to build up steam.

About 60 people were on board at 6:40 a.m. when the *Gazelle*'s engineer, Moses Toner, jumped off the boat, on to dock, and took off running. About a minute later, both boilers exploded and blew the vessel apart, killing 24 people and seriously injuring another 30, 4 of whom died later. The coroner's jury blamed the engineer of overloading the boiler's firebox with cordwood. The engineer had vanished and was never brought to justice.

The sidewheeler *Wallamet* had been lying alongside *Gazelle*, her works were seriously damaged, and her pilot J.M. Pudge was killed in the explosion. The whole town of Canemah came running to the rescue, and boats had to be launched to save the living people and recover the bodies floating in the river. Captain Hereford was injured but survived.

The wreck was bought by Captains R. Hoyt, William Wells, and A. S. Murray, and was taken down over the falls on August 11, 1855. They repaired and changed her into a new steamship, the *Sarah Hoyt* and then she was later named the *Senorita*. The warehouse company afterwards built the *Oregon*, which later sunk and proved a total loss. The property passed into other hands, the buildings were later burned down, and all was swept away in the flood of December of 1861.

Many years later a memorial plaque was placed on a rock overlooking the Willamette River and the deserted Canemah landing, which stated:

600 YARDS SOUTH OF THIS POINT,
EXPLOSION OF STEAMER GAZELLE. APRIL 8, 1854.
LOSS OF TWENTY FOUR LIVES.
MARKED MAY 13TH, 1933 BY MULTNOMAH CHAPTER D. A. R.
(Photo by Daniel S. Cowan)

Sternwheelers could work from Astoria and Portland upriver of the Columbia as far as the Celilo Falls. These waterfalls have a twenty-foot drop over a ledge of basalt. Beyond the falls are the Tenmile Rapids, filled with half of a mile of raging currents, as well as the Fivemile Rapids which stretched for 1 ½ miles. Combined, they constricted this run of the Columbia River between sharp rock walls less than three hundred feet apart. Past the Big Eddy and Threemile Rapids, the waters calm just above the town of The Dalles.

The first sternwheeler operating on the Upper Willamette River was the *Enterprise* (not to be confused with many other steamers by the same name), built in the fall of 1855 by Archibald Jamieson, Captain A. S. Murray, Armory Holbrook, and John Torrance. She was 115 feet in length, 15 feet in width, and had sizeable cabin rooms. From 1855 to 1858, the sternwheeler worked on the Willamette River between Oregon City, Canemah, and Corvallis. Corvallis was thought to be the leading point on the Willamette. Traders above Corvallis tried to get Captain Jamieson to bring the *Enterprise* closer but he would not go farther than Orleans, then a small community on the east side of the river across from Corvallis. Even though the *Enterprise* was the first truly valuable boat on that part of the river, in July of 1858, Jamieson sold her to Captain Thomas A. Wright. Jamieson used the money from the sale to build another steamer, the *Onward*.

Captain Tom Wright's plan for *Enterprise* was to take her up north into British waters to work in the Fraser Gold Rush. Before she could go, he had to move her from the upper to the lower Willamette River by lining the vessel over the Willamette Falls. Steamboats could not navigate the water. (Captain Jamieson was later killed when a vessel under his command was accidentally swept over the falls and destroyed). Lining was a practice where a heavy cable was attached to the boat, and then to a well anchored windlass on shore. Slowly the cable would be let out to allow the vessel to gradually pass over the falls to the lower river.

Captain Wright then took the *Enterprise* down the lower Willamette and Columbia Rivers to Astoria. Once he got there, Wright arranged for an oceangoing ship to tow them to Victoria, B.C. He left Astoria with her under tow, but the strong breakers on the Columbia Bar triggered the *Enterprise* to rock so hard that she leaked. Captain Wright got her to into shallow water in Astoria before she sank. She was raised and repaired, and they started their journey again in August.

The *Enterprise*, along with other American steamboats, got licenses from the governor of British Columbia to run in British territory. She was the second steam-powered vessel to work on the Fraser River.

The year of 1853 was not good for the Northwest steamboat trade. Although many boats were both imported and built in and near Oregon City, none of them panned out for profit. The *Wallamet*, a huge sidewheeler, 272 gross tons, 150 feet in length, with a 23-foot beam, twin smoke stacks, and 5 feet draft was built in Canemah in 1853. There were sixty staterooms in the sidewheeler's upper saloon. She was modeled after the Mississippi river boats and built by John T. Thomas for J. McCrosky.

She was launched on August 11, at Canemah. There were about 50-60 men on board at the time of her launch. She became the fourth steamer working out of Canemah.

Unfortunately, this southern style of boat wasn't practical for the Oregon rivers. After working her on the Willamette River for more than a year, the men made no profit. In September 1854, the *Wallamet* was sold and towed south to California, but she did not last long there. She was used on both the Sacramento and San Joaquin Rivers. She was dismantled in 1860. She had been a good steamer, but could not match either the speed or comfort of the *Lot Whitcomb*.

The sidewheeler *Belle of Oregon City* was a very distinguished steamer. She was the first iron hulled steamboat built on the west coast of North America. She was completely constructed in Oregon in 1853. Her material, from the engines and iron sheets that shaped her hull, all of her machinery, to the bell, came entirely from Oregon City at a foundry owned by Thomas V. Smith. Smith had come out to Oregon from Baltimore and set up his own business. He created the first iron steamboat built entirely on the Pacific Coast. Captain William H. Troup built the steamer for Captains W. B. Wells and Richard Williams. The *Belle* was 90 feet long, with a 16-foot beam where a deck with wide guards gave her an overall length of 96 feet. She had plenty of room for her side wheels.

Captains Williams and Wells put the *Belle* on the Portland to Oregon City route on the Willamette River, with passenger fares for only $2 each way. She would leave from Oregon City by 8:00 a.m., stopping at Milwaukie by 8:30, and reach Portland by around 9:30. At 2 p.m. each day, the *Belle* steamed back upriver, reaching the Willamette Falls again by 4 p.m. Since the water was so shallow on the Willamette near the mouth of the Clackamas River, known as the Clackamas Rapids, only smaller draft boats could make this run. She also worked on the Cowlitz River and to Fort Vancouver.

The *Belle* increased her routes from the Columbia River to the lower Cascades, three runs a week, under Captain Wells. J. M. Gilman was the engineer and N. B. Ingalls was the purser. Passengers would board the *Belle*, then disembark at the lower Cascades, connect onto the portage road along the north bank, then board the sidewheeler, *Mary* upriver to the next head of navigation at The Dalles. Freight charges were expensive at $50 a ton on cargo from Portland to The Dalles, but *Belle* and *Mary* still could not keep up with the demand, and other crafts came on the routes, driving rates down to $30 a ton.

When the Oregon Steam navigation Company was created, the *Belle* became part of their line of boats used on the Columbia River. With so many crafts, the new company rarely used the *Belle*.

Because the *Belle* was made of iron, she was much more durable than the other early Oregon steamers. She worked up through 1869 and was finally scrapped; her iron was sent to China and her engines, though barely operating, went to power a sawmill at Oak Point.

Soon after the sale of the *Lot Whitcomb*, the *Jennie Clark* was built in February of 1855. The *Jennie Clark* was the first steam-powered sternwheeler to travel the Columbia River with passengers. She was different from the other steamers on the waterway because she had her wheel at the stern. Crafted by master builder Jacob Kamm, the *Jennie Clark* was first class from the pilothouse to her keel. Almost immediately, Captain John C. Ainsworth, who he had met earlier, joined Kamm and both men decided that the sternwheeler was superior to propeller driven and sidewheeler boats. Propellers were too susceptible to the rough waters as well as very expensive to fix when the shafts from rocks and other obstacles in the river damaged them. The men modified the design for the *Jennie Clark* to cope with the shallow conditions for which sidewheelers were unfit; she was the archetype of the future Columbia River designs. The stern paddle wheels gave a stronger pushing power than the propellers or sidewheels. They needed less "dip" or submergence in ratio to draft. They were flat bottomed, requiring only two or three feet of water and could slip over sandbars.

Kamm oversaw as much of her building as possible. Her hull and upper works were built in Milwaukie, Oregon Territory, while her engines were assembled in Baltimore, Maryland to Kamm's specifications. He paid $1,663.16 and had them shipped to the West Coast at a cost of another $1,030.02. Finished, she was 115 feet long and an 18 ½-foot beam, 50 gross tons, with a 4-foot hold. On her hull was a single cabin, in which the boiler was centered, with the engines aft to reach the wheel. Even though Kamm didn't approve of it, her passenger cabin was placed forward of the boiler.

She was launched in February of 1855, with Ainsworth as her first captain. He was pleased with her smooth glide over the Columbia and how she securely pushed through the water with efficient speed. Both he and Kamm turned her over to the Abernathy and Clark Company carrying the daily mail between Portland and Oregon City. The *Jennie Clark* soon became known as a fast and comfortable sternwheeler.

In July of 1862, a new field of steamboat business was developing on the Columbia River. The population and prosperity kept growing in Portland and soon people wanted to take their vacations at the coast. The *Jennie Clark* became the first regular seaside vessel from Portland. For a round trip fare of only $15, the Oregon Steam Navigation Company put the *Jennie Clark* in service every week from Portland to Fort Clatsop. When the *Jennie Clark* came south, she did not stop in Astoria, but turned into Young's Bay and treaded up the Lewis & Clark River to Fort Clatsop. Once there her passengers could hire horses or carriages for the quick trip through the forest to Clatsop Beach, or if they wished, they could walk the short distance to the shore. Because she had few passengers, she was dismantled in 1863, her engine transferred to the *Forty-Nine*. Ironically, by the 1870s there were hundreds of customers traveling to and from Portland and Astoria.

Another popular sternwheeler in Oregon City was the *Carrie Ladd*, which was built in Milwaukie by John T. Thomas for Jacob Kamm, Captain John Ainsworth and others in 1858. She was named after a Portland banker's daughter. The banker had helped arrange the financing for the Oregon Steam Navigation Company (which later held a monopoly on steam navigation on the Columbia River). She was launched in October of 1858.

The *Carrie Ladd* was one of the first steamboats specifically built with the Columbia River in mind, which made her different from most other steamboats. Instead of a compilation of castoff hulls, engines, or machinery from earlier vessels, she was built from scratch. Although she was not particularly large (her dimensions were 126 feet in length, with a 24-foot 4-inch beam, and a 4 ½-foot depth of hold), she had powerful engines, and was most likely the best of the steamboats built in Oregon in the 1850s. Her design became the essential draft of the Columbia River steamboat, which would later be used throughout the Pacific Northwest, British Columbia, Alaska, and the Yukon.

Under the command of Captain Ainsworth, she took her first trip on a run to Vancouver and the Cascades on February 9, 1859. It took the *Carrie Ladd* 1 hour and 25 minutes for the 16 miles from Portland to Vancouver. It was then 5 hours and 44 minutes to go the 53 miles from Portland to the lower Cascades. The return trip to Portland took 4 hours 38 minutes. Her entire voyage took her less than 12 hours, a very impressive speed for the time.

Although the *Carrie Ladd* was originally built for Oregon City to work under the Union Transportation Company, the forerunner of the Oregon Steam Navigation Company, she had so much power they moved her to the Cascades. She could easily carry over three hundred passengers a trip. She had no difficulty in going right up to the foot of the rapids. The *Carrie Ladd* got a good share of the Columbia River traffic, more than any other steamer.

When the *Julia Barclay*, a steamer from Puget Sound was brought to the Columbia River, there was a short period of competition on the Portland - Cascades route. This was resolved when the OSNC bought the *Julia*. In the early 1860s, both sternwheelers ran interchangeably, each carrying from two hundred to three hundred passengers every voyage.

On June 3, 1862, while in the command of Captain James Strang, the *Carrie Ladd* struck a rock 18 miles below the Cascades on the Columbia River, near Cape Horn, Washington, and sank. The *Mountain Buck* safely rescued the passengers. Although the *Carrie Ladd* was raised and repaired, she was never as strong of a boat for the gorge work. In 1864, she was converted into a barge: her engines were used in the *Nez Perce Chief* and other parts went to the *Mountain Queen.*

Even with the steady improvements and inventions in sternwheeler layouts, the boats couldn't easily get past the Columbia River's large amounts of silt left after her natural flow at high volume, usually occurring in the spring and early summer. Just after the Civil War, in 1866, the first channel improvement project took place along the Columbia River basin. The U.S. Army Engineers cleared several snags that flowed in from the Willamette River. Dredging the estuary began in 1873. The success of these developments started the proposal for large channels along the rivers.

The demand for commercial routing on the Columbia River began around 1877 when Congress agreed to build a channel from the Portland/Vancouver area to the mouth of the river. That same year, maps were completed for the Cascades Canal past the Cascade Rapids 45 miles east of Portland. The plan was for the Army Engineers to build a canal 7,200 feet long and 50 feet wide with two locks, that would be eight foot deep at low water by 70 feet wide and 300 feet long. Because the region had to be defined within the developed jurisdiction, the construction for the Cascade Locks Navigation did not start until November of 1878. The canal was not completed until November 5, 1896, as lack of funds and labor, engineering and building snags and other unforeseen setbacks slowed the work.

For the first time, the Columbia River was safe for travel through the treacherous falls of the Cascades. Beforehand, steamers could only run the river during low water. At other times of the year, the rapids were too dangerous. Still not completely finished when opened, the Canal had already cost $3.7 million, more than double the original estimate. On November 5, 1896, steamboats carried several hundred people through the locks to view the work. The steamer *Sarah Dixon* fired cannon salutes throughout the day.

The canal was an instant benefit for the river. Between 1898 and 1920, the value of freight through the canal surpassed the cost of construction. The locks and canal were used until 1938 when they were covered over by the water behind Bonneville Dam. The dam included a lock for river traffic.

The dedication of the dam was celebrated with the passage of the only oceangoing steamship, the 300-foot *Charles L. Wheeler, Jr.* of San Francisco, which made the trip from Portland to The Dalles. The steamer took 1,420 tons of general cargo up for delivery and took back about 1,000 tons. Captain Arthur Riggs piloted it, the same man who took the *J. N. Teal* to Lewiston, Idaho, in 1915 when the Celilo Canal was opened. The Dalles community and the Inland Empire thought this might be the beginning of a regular ocean service for their town, but this would not be so. No other oceangoing commercial steamer ever came that way.

On March 20, 1947, the last steamer to make the passage from Portland to The Dalles (before the *Portland*'s restoration) was the *Georgie Burton* that had been retired from the Western Fleet. She carried the maiden name of Mrs. Georgie Pittock, whose husband had been the primary owner and publisher of the newspaper, the *Oregonian*, and a director of the Western Towing & Navigation Company. The *Georgie Burton* was originally built in Portland in 1886 with the name *N. S. Bentley*, and then later named the *Albany*. She was rebuilt, extending her length from 150 to 153 feet and renamed again in 1906 when Western bought her for pushing barges and towing logs.

She was given to The Dalles for service in a proposed marine park along the riverfront. There she remained until the enormous Memorial Day flood of 1948. She had been left forgotten, docked along the concrete wall of the canal. When a huge wave smashed her into the heavy barge next to her, her hull was broken and the house collapsed, with parts of her washing down the river.

The Columbia River near the Vancouver crested at 30 feet, the highest stage since the late 1800s, and the discharge was about 1 million cubic feet per second for almost a month. At least 15 people died in the flood, and the city was a total loss. Flooding also occurred in several other communities downriver of Portland and Vancouver on both the Oregon and Washington banks of the river.

Rebuilt in 1906, this 150-foot long steam-powered sternwheeler, the Georgie Burton, as shown here in Portland. (Larry Barber Collection)

Here is the steam sternwheeler, the Gov. Newell and another unidentified steamer with a water crane undertow. She was built in Portland during the year of 1883 and dismantled in 1900. She was 206 tons with a 112-foot length. This photo was taken on the Willamette River from the 8th St. dock in Oregon City.

(Oregon Maritime Museum Collection)

MINNIE HILL:
THE FIRST WOMAN STEAMBOAT CAPTAIN ON THE WEST COAST

(Oregon State Library Collection)

Minnie May Mossman was born in Albany, Oregon, on July 20, 1863, the daughter of Isaac Van Dorsey Mossman, of Dutch descent, who pioneered the pony express lines in Oregon and Washington before the Civil War period. She was the second daughter of seven children, and quickly learned to take charge of a large family. When she turned 18 years old, she took a teaching job in Portland, Oregon. There she met a dashing young river man, Charles Oliver Hill. They married on February 25, 1883.

Charles was born in New York in 1855 to a successful merchant family. With the death of his mother before his first birthday, Charles was put into an orphanage in New Jersey. When he was 12, he ran away from there and worked his way across America looking for good work and new adventures. He ended up in Seattle, Washington, and worked in the timber industry until he boarded a steamer heading up north for the mining country in Alaska where he worked until he turned 25 years old.

Charles came south to Portland and found work as a deckhand on the sternwheeler *Toledo*, which ran between Portland and the Cowlitz River. Hill soon became mate and studied for his pilot license, which he earned in October of 1884. His first command was on the *A. A. McCully*, a 148-foot long steamer sternwheeler. During this time, Minnie and Charles were married and worked on the river together.

It was while he and Minnie were working on the Cowlitz River that they discovered an old 30-foot river sloop *Jehu*, one of the last of the river sailing boats, tied up in Monticello (now Longview, Washington) The couple purchased the sloop and changed it into a working vessel. They cut it in half and added 10 feet to the middle of the hull. They installed two small engines, a sternwheel, cabin, and pilothouse and named it the *Minnie Hill*. It began operations as a trader boat on the lower Columbia River, between Rainier and Cathlamet. It was such a light scow, that it could not buck a strong ebb tide, so the Hills had to plan all trips with the roll of the tide in mind.

As their business grew, the *Minnie Hill* worked along the harbors in Portland delivering goods and farm products between the settlers and the city. They would stop along Rainier, Cathlamet and out of the way tributaries and sloughs to meet the needs of their customers.

Minnie had been working with her husband on various boats for several years; she knew about planking, caulking, boiler firing, engine controls, and the skills of navigation and piloting. Soon she learned and mastered the craft of piloting steamboats. The testing was extremely difficult for her as the examiners wanted to refuse her a license with no justification. Yet, even with the scowling board of inspectors, she earned her master's license to run steamboats on Dec. 1, 1886, and succeeded as the first licensed woman to command a steamer on the Columbia River; she remained the only woman licensed as an operator until 1907. Minnie opened the way for another woman in the Puget Sound area to receive a second-class master's license.

The floating market was successful for several years. Crowds would hear about the *Minnie Hill* approaching and they waited to watch a beautiful female captain dock the boat. Aside from her nautical intelligence, Minnie became a skilled sales person. She would wear new bonnets, dresses, parasols, and other merchandise that might attract women shoppers. Often sales were made as soon as Captain Hill pulled into the landing. It was told that sometimes when Minnie returned to Portland, she might be only wearing rags or a hand stitched flour sack garment because she had sold the clothes she had worn.

One problem Minnie had was with the lack of the English language and dialects of many foreign and native American women who wanted to buy her merchandise. She had to interpret their body language and gestures and there was also much haggling and bargaining before she could make a profitable sale, but they did pay off. The Hills made around $22,000 in cash until they sold the *Minnie Hill* in 1889, and moved up to a larger vessel. (The man who bought the *Minnie Hill* used it as a floating saloon, something that was not approved of by the Hills. They felt relieved a year later when they learned that a drunken man had accidentally set fire to the *Minnie Hill* and it was completely destroyed.)

The new steamer sternwheeler became Minnie's favorite working rig. Bought from J. C. Trullinger, the *Gov. Newell* had been built in Portland for the Shoalwater Bay Transportation Company. She was 112 feet in length, a 20-foot beam with a 5-foot hold, and 206 gross tons with engines 12 by 48 inches. With the *Gov. Newell*, the Hills specialized in moving scows filled with jetty stone from Fisher's quarry, 15 miles east of Vancouver, Washington. They would navigate downstream to meet the U.S. Army Engineer's towboat *Cascades* just below Vancouver where they would trade empty barges for the full ones and then take the loads down to Astoria. The stone was used to build the great south jetty at the mouth of the Columbia River.

Minnie had added duties now with her new steamer. She now had a crew of eight men to direct: the deckhands, engineers, firefighters, one Chinese cook, a pilot and her husband. Portland now had three bridges overpassing the Willamette River that added to her anxieties.

One of Minnie's most difficult experiences was the day when the Willamette River was running high and stormy. As the boat moved towards the first bridge, the scow on the starboard side abruptly capsized, spilling its load into the water. It rolled up empty with one end low in the river, the other rising high above the pilothouse. Minnie fought the current to keep her steamer under control and successfully went under the bridge without touching, and then she steered straight through the other two bridges safe and sound.

Another memorable task was on a cold morning in November of 1893 when the *Gov. Newell* was tied up in her berth at the foot of Jefferson Street on the Willamette River in Portland. A westbound Hawthorne Avenue streetcar with 30 passengers skidded on the icy rails of the Madison Street Bridge while it was opening to let the steamer *Elwood* pass through, bound for Oregon City. The streetcar broke through the gates and went crashing down into the river. Nearly 20 people escaped and swam to the surface. While rescuers were picking up these wet survivors, both Minnie and Charles launched a small boat from the *Gov. Newell* to search for the missing ten, but several were drowned.

Captain Minnie ran the *Gov. Newell* for fourteen years while Captain Charles Hill took charge as engineer in the engine room; also during this time she had given birth to two children but only one survived. When the *Gov. Newell* became too worn to continue working, Captain Hill retired along with her. She had her boat dismantled in 1900 and went back home to become a full time housewife and mother. Occasionally over the next two years she made trips as captain on their sternwheelers the 118-foot *Tahoma*, the 102-foot *Paloma*, and the 140-foot *Glenola* whenever an emergency arose that left a boat temporarily without a captain.

A few years after Minnie's retirement, Charles set up a lumbering business and created the Hill Logging Company in Lewis Company, Washington. From the logging company, the town of Bunker was established. The mill was situated near the Chehalis river and ran both a sawmill and a shingle mill. Donkeys and steam locomotives were used to haul and ship the logs to Tacoma and other nearby mills in the area. In 1910, Charles was listed as president of the logging camp and continued in that work for some time. A fire in April of 1919 destroyed the sawmill, but the company continued to ship logs and Charles was still manager until one year later when the business stopped operations and the company was closed.

During their careers, the Hills owned and worked six steamboats, the *Minnie Hill, Clatsop Chief, Gov. Newell, Tahoma, Paloma*, and *Glenola*. Charles died in Portland in 1944 at the age of 89 and Minnie passed away two years later at the age of 83.

Minnie avoided publicity throughout her career, even when authors of national status requested the honor of writing her story. At least two movie producers tried to get her to allow them to write a film about her life, but she refused. Her son Herbert Wells Hill, born in Portland on September 19, 1894, was the only living person who knew her life, both as a boat captain and a mother. Herbert Hill died in Portland on June 12, 1942.

The People's Transportation Company soon had a competing line of steamboats on the river by 1862. Most of these vessels were designed to attract commerce from the Oregon Steam Navigation Company, emerging from its 1860 incorporation to become a developed monopoly of transport along the northwest rivers. (The OSNC was the direct descendant of the Union Transportation Company of 1859.)

Railroad industrialist Ben Holladay bought the People's Transportation Company in 1871. Soon afterward, Holladay suffered financial difficulties and sold his holdings to the OSNC, completing the circle that began more than a decade earlier; it became Oregon's first true monopoly.

With its stranglehold on river traffic and portage routes at The Dalles and Celilo, the OSNC could charge nearly whatever it wanted for passage, and it did. For example, the company charged the user fee of $120 a ton for freight to Lewiston, and a "ton" was a measure of cubic feet, not weight. The company's price on the Columbia River was about 10 times what it charged on the Missouri River, and there was no choice but to pay it. In 1864, with the Idaho gold rush at its height, the OSNC made a huge profit of $783,339. (That is approximately $45 million in today's dollars.) The OSNC tolerated many attacks over its rates and profits. In 1882, a railroad was completed between Celilo and Wallula, offering southeastern Washington farmers hope they would avoid expensive steamboats for carrying their wheat downriver to Portland. Unfortunately, the company that built the line was an auxiliary of the OSNC, so they kept their monopoly on transportation along the Columbia. This was long before government regulation of interstate commerce.

Located near the union of the Willamette and Columbia Rivers, the Columbia Slough gave the city of Portland a profitable base for sternwheel companies. (Larry Barber Collection)

51

The Ocklahama is guiding a ship on the Willamette River through a series of bridges.   (Shaver Transportation Collection)

By 1896, the Oregon Railroad and Navigation Company had purchased and added enough smaller railroad companies and became the primary train system, operating a rail network of 1,143 miles of track running east from Portland to Washington and northern Idaho. The Oregon Railway and Navigation Company's purchase of the Oregon Steam Navigation Company in 1880 gave it a limited route on the Oregon side of the Columbia River. In the transaction, they got nearly every valuable sternwheeler on the Columbia. The commercial boats that changed hands included the *Wide West, Emma Hayward, S.G. Reed, Fannie Patton, S.T. Church, McMinnville, Ocklahama, E.N. Cook, Governor Grover, Alice, Bonita, Dixie Thompson, Welcome, R.R. Thompson, Mountain Queen, Idaho, Annie Faxon, Jon Gates, Harvest Queen, Spokane, New Tenino, Almota, Willamette Chief, Orient, Occident, Bonanza, Champion,* and *D.S. Baker.*

The steamboating trade was drastically changing. Railroads were slowly driving down the competition of many sternwheelers, some of which just ran out of business. Sternwheelers still had the say while operating on the Snake River, but they were mostly connecting with the railheads at Riparia and Pasco, Washington.

The company continued to increase its expansion of the Columbia River route, surveying from where the Oregon Steam Navigation tracks ended at Celilo and continuing up east to Wallula. By 1882, the route along the Columbia River was finished. (As early as 1880, the main competitor of the Oregon Railway and

Navigation Company was the Shaver Transportation Company - which still works in Portland today.)

Other steamboats were built in this period as well. These included the *Mary* and the *Wasco* in 1854 and 1855, both constructed above the Cascades for service between the Cascades and The Dalles. The *Colonel Wright*, built in 1858, was the first steamboat launched there. This boat was assembled at the mouth of the Deschutes River and was used to carry freight between Celilo and old Fort Walla Walla near the union of the Walla Walla River and the Columbia. In the following year, the *Colonel Wright* probed 50 miles up the Snake River. The year after that it became the first steamboat to reach Lewiston, Idaho. During the Idaho gold rush of 1861, the ship went up the Clearwater to within 12 miles of its forks, or about 30 miles above Lewiston. Two other boats joined the upper river trade in 1860, the *Tenino* and the sternwheeler *Okanogan.*

The new and upcoming Columbia River steamboats were designed and built specifically to cope with the layout of northwest rivers. Their hulls were long and narrow, their draft slight. Some carried as many as five hundred passengers, crowded into every available inch of space, and hauled as much as five hundred tons of freight.

Many of these newly built steamboats were used all around the northwest, such as the *Eliza Anderson*, which was built by the Columbia River Steam Navigation Company and launched on November 27, 1858, in Portland, Oregon. She was a sidewheeler driven by a low-pressure boiler generating steam for a single cylinder walking beam steam engine. She was built completely of wood, measuring 197 feet long, with a 25.5-foot beam, and rated at 276 tons capacity.

After her trial run on the lower Willamette and Columbia Rivers, she was sold to an association of John T. Bradford, several Canadian stockholders and three brothers, Tom, John T. and George S. Wright, who were early steamboat workers in the Pacific Northwest. Under the command of Captain J. G. Hustler, she was brought around to Victoria, Canada in March of 1859. Because of the Fraser River Gold Rush, there was a scarcity of steamboats in British Columbia between 1858 and 1859. By March 30, the *Anderson* had completed two round trips to Fort Langley, and returned to Victoria carrying $40,000 in gold dust.

The *Eliza Anderson* worked from 1858 to 1898 mostly on Puget Sound, the Strait of Georgia, and the Fraser River. She also had a brief time up in Alaska. Once she arrived back in Olympia, her owners put her on the Olympia - Victoria mail run during August of 1859. Her agent, John H. Scranton, who had the mail contract, coordinated this. The *Eliza Anderson*, also known as the *Old Anderson*, was thought to be a slow and underpowered steamship for her time. Even so, she played a valuable role in the Underground Railroad as well as her reckless last voyage to Alaska as part of the Klondike Gold Rush.

On September 24, 1860, Charles Mitchell, a 14-year-old black male, hid on board the *Eliza Anderson*, hoping to get to Canada to escape slavery. He had been working on the steamer, and another older black man working on the *Anderson* as a "temporary steward" had helped him find a hiding place on the boat. He was discovered at either Steilacoom or Seattle, and because he promised to work off his passage, they did not lock him up. Once in Victoria, word got out that Mitchell was being held against his will aboard the *Anderson*. A group of protesters made up of both white and black citizens of Victoria marched down to the dock. A lawyer presented a petition for a writ of habeas corpus to Chief Justice Cameron, who granted the writ. Mitchell was removed from the steamer by the Canadian authorities and became a free man.

When things were winding down for the *Eliza Anderson* on the Olympia - Victoria route, she was tied up to Percival Dock in Olympia for some time, until the Cassiar Gold Rush in northern British Columbia offered miners a chance to make money. She then was fixed up to make voyages as far north as Wrangell, Alaska. When the gold rush died out, the *Anderson* was returned to Seattle, where she lay between 1877 and 1883, eventually sinking at her moorings.

Here is the Eliza Anderson moored on the Willamette River in Portland, Oregon in 1859. (Oregon Maritime Museum Collection)

In 1883, Captain Wright raised the *Eliza Anderson*, pumped her out, scrubbed her up, and put her on the run from Seattle to New Westminster, British Columbia, with Captain E. W. Holmes in command and O. O. Denny as her chief engineer. By this time, the Oregon Railway and Navigation Company was trying to monopolize all water and rail transport in the state of Oregon and the Washington Country. This brought on a rate war. The *Anderson* ran fares down to $1.00 and was beating both the *Olympian* and the sidewheeler *Geo. E. Starr*, until she was seized by the customs collector, Captain H. F. Beecher, on charges of bringing in immigrants contrary to the Chinese Exclusion Act. Captain Wright could clear himself of these charges, but with the *Anderson* having been off the route so long, his competitors had captured all the business. It was said that this broke Captain Wright's heart and his investments. In October of 1886, Captain Wright sold the *Anderson* to the Puget Sound and Alaska Steamship Company, which ran her under Captain J. W. Tarte on the Victoria route again. As late as 1888 she was involved in a steamboat race with another old vessel, the sidewheeler steam tug *Goliath*. That time the *Goliath*, still in her prime, took the challenge, but lost the race. The *Anderson* stayed on the Puget Sound under the Northwestern Steamship Company, which was managed by Captain Daniel Bachhelder Jackson.

In 1890, the *Eliza Anderson* was laid up on the Duwamish River during the financial crisis of the early 1890s. She would have just rotted away there except for the discovery of gold in the Yukon Territory. Gold miners were willing to book passages on just about anything that floated, and the *Anderson*, which had been tied up for quite some time, soon became a roadhouse and gambling hall. Along with many other boats, the *Anderson* became a "floating coffin," a place of gambling, dancing, and crime. Once her stint as an illegal casino was over, the Moran shipyard in Seattle purchased her and did a quick overhaul and she was back in the water on July 31, 1897.

On August 10, 1897, she began her voyage to Alaska under Captain Thomas Powers with about 40 passengers, including a few women and children. The plan was to take an entire fleet up to St. Michael, the only port anywhere near the mouth of the Yukon River, leave the *Eliza Anderson* there, and take the steamer *Merwin* up the Yukon to the gold fields. The trip was from the start a disaster. *Anderson*'s owners had oversold her tickets, and the passengers, finding tight space aboard, much less than they had been promised, were kept from throwing the purser overboard by Captain Powers. Shortly after departure, it was found that the *Anderson* was missing much of her basic sea going equipment, such as a compass. Fights broke out among the passengers and the crew. When the *Anderson* arrived in Connex, British Columbia, coal loading by her bungling crew caused her to swing out of control into the ship *Glory of the Seas*, causing minor damage to one of her paddle guards.

Finally, the convoy reached Kodiak, Alaska, which had been a very long sea voyage from St. Michael. There, as the *Eliza Anderson* took on coal, five passengers got off and refused to reboard, convinced that the *Anderson* would sink on the way. The boats ran into a gale near Kodiak Island and the *Merwin*'s towline broke off and fell into the water. Sixteen unlucky passengers aboard the *Anderson* were barely rescued by the steamer *Holyoke*.

The *Holyoke, Merwin,* and *Bryant* all had moved away from the *Eliza Anderson;* when they arrived at Dutch Harbor, they reported her missing. The revenue cutter *Corwin* went out to look for the lost sidewheeler. The *Anderson* had run out of coal in the middle of the storm. Her crew had not bothered to fully load the ship with coal in Kodiak. They had just hidden the bags they were supposed to haul on board and heave into the coal bins. While they were stranded, both the crew and passengers were forced to burn the wooden coal bunkers, and finally the cabin furniture and even the cabin partitions. Passengers were writing notes to loved ones and tossing them overboard in bottles, of which there was an abundant supply since most of the boat's stock of whisky had been consumed to keep up morale.

The *Eliza Anderson* was forced to run for shelter: Kodiak Island. By chance, she found an unused cannery on the island, which had 75 tons of coal in the warehouse. The *Anderson*'s company quickly snatched this supply, and with it, the boat somehow made it to Dutch Harbor.

Following a steam pipe blast and crashing into a dock in Dutch Harbor, the passengers and crew vacated her. During a terrible storm early in March of 1898, she broke from her anchorage and proceeded ashore before any help could be given her. She was left lying on her side, with the tide flowing through several jagged holes in her base. The news of the *Eliza Anderson*'s wreck was brought to Seattle by the steamer *Bertha*. Her wreck in Alaska is a fitting end to her 41-year career since she had so many times been rescued from the boneyard and put back into commission.

The peak of faster, more reliable boats came with the steaming of the big boats of the 1880s: the *Telephone, T. J. Potter,* and the *Bailey Gatzert*. When they blew their whistles coming out of Portland, cutting the river on either side, leaving long rolling waves going towards the shore and a straight swath of froth behind as their wheels reversed, people onshore watched and admired them. These steamers were elegant, long and narrow, with their tall stacks spilling a stream of smoke, all carrying a banner with their name on the jack staff, and the national insignia at the king post, or stern.

The Bailey Gatzert is heading towards the Cascade Locks from Portland in 1901. She is traveling along the Columbia River. (Oregon Maritime Museum Collection)

The *Bailey Gatzert* (named after a Seattle mayor) was built in 1890 in John Holland's shipyard in Seattle for the Seattle Steam and Navigation Company. She was 177 feet 3 inches in length, with a 32-foot beam, and an 8-foot depth of hold. She had a poppet valve engine 22 by 84 inches and a net tonnage of 444.32. Even though she was ready to work, she didn't get to the Columbia River until 1892. She was the first steamer built to carry passengers as earlier vessels traveling along the Columbia River Gorge area were used for transporting freight. She was a fast wood fueled sternwheeler, displaying her graceful hull going to and from Portland, Astoria, The Dalles, and the lower Cascades.

The *Bailey Gatzert* was considered one of the speediest steamers on the Columbia; other captains would try to race past her on their daily routes but usually they couldn't keep up. She could travel from The Dalles to Portland in just over five hours. In 1887, she had to give up her notoriety to the *Telephone*, which became the fastest sternwheeler in the world.

The new *Bailey Gatzert* was declared the finest sternwheeler craft afloat. Composers Henry Decker and Richard Velguth wrote a piano melody to commemorate her. Fisher Music Co. in Portland, Oregon, published it in 1902.

They called it "The Bailey Gatzert March." It was performed during the 1905 Lewis and Clark Exposition and Oriental Fair in Portland. During the fair, the *Bailey Gatzert* made twice daily runs from Portland to the Cascade Locks.

The *Bailey Gatzert* was reconstructed in 1907 and bore no resemblance to the first boat. The new sternwheeler, of the Regulator Line steamers, was launched on August 24, 1907, at the Portland Shipbuilding Company. Her lines were entirely different from the original and the rooms on the hurricane deck had been removed. The *Bailey Gatzert*'s hull was lengthened by 19 feet 3 inches and she was trimmed like a steam schooner. Her cylinder and all the timbers in her hull were of the finest wood and she was able to stand the steam she produced. She was granted a license for about 350 passengers and an excursion permit of 625.

The sternwheeler was returned to Seattle in 1917 to work as a car and passenger ferry. In the 1920s, she was altered at Todd Shipyards in Seattle. She was sponsoned out (widened) and fitted with an elevator to load and unload cars. She could carry about 25 vehicles and became the first automobile ferry on the Seattle - Bremerton route. In 1926, the *Bailey Gatzert* was taken out of service; her hull was converted to a floating machine shop in Lake Union, Washington.

The first *Telephone* sternwheeler was built in 1885 at the foot of the Jefferson Bridge in Portland, near the same time the telephone exchange was opened in Astoria. Captain U. B. Scott and associates, who called themselves the Columbia River and Puget Sound Navigation Company, designed her. She was 172 feet long, 386 gross tons, and was put together for the passenger and freight service on both the Columbia and Willamette Rivers to replace the *Fleetwood*, a small screw propelled 111-foot in length tug. The *Fleetwood* had been assembled in Portland in 1881, but was transferred to Puget Sound in 1888.

On July 2, 1884, full of passengers and cargo, Captain Scott took her from Portland to Astoria, 110 miles, in less than 4 ½ hours, making the round trip in 11 hours and 4 minutes. At that time 25 miles an hour was a record breaking speed. Captain Scott's design became well known all along the west coast.

In 1903, J. S. Cochran rebuilt the third Telephone for the Arrow navigation Co. of Puget Sound, Washington. (Oregon Maritime Museum Collection)

Sadly, on November 12, 1887, the *Telephone* caught fire from an oil backfire from the boiler just as she was coming into Astoria. Captain Scott forced the steamer, blazing flames over the evening sky, towards shore just below Tongue Point near Upper Astoria. The engineer kicked off the throttle at full speed while the crew fought the persistent inferno. The *Telephone* struck at 20 mph and skidded across the flats sustaining little damage to her hull. Captain Scott saved all but one of his 140 passengers and 32 crew members, but the boat and cargo burned to the waterline within just a few minutes. The *Telephone* was towed back to Portland and reconstructed into another sternwheeler.

The second *Telephone* went into service in 1888. She was 200 feet long and 500 gross tons. On a foggy night in 1892, she sank near the mouth of the Willamette River. Her passengers were transferred to Coon Island. She was raised and restored to continue service until 1899 when her engines were removed for a new *Telephone* steamer.

The third *Telephone* was built in 1903, and except for three summer months of 1905, she was seldom used. J. S. Cochran of the Arrow Navigation Co. of Puget Sound rebuilt her. Her tonnage was raised to 794 gross tons; she was 201.5 feet long, with a 31.5 feet beam, and an 8-foot depth of hold, with engines 26" x 96".

During those years, she was a landmark at the Haseltine dock on the east side of Portland. She was known to be then the fastest sternwheeler afloat. Even with her many jobs, she was a high maintenance steamer. The stockholders of the Arrow Navigation Co. refused to put any more money into her. The *Telephone* was returned to Captain Scott. In 1907, she was chartered to the Regulator Line and worked between Portland and The Dalles. She was put in service to replace the steamer *Joseph Kellogg*, which had been returned to her previous owners. She was later sold to The Dalles, Portland, and Astoria Navigation Company. In 1909, she was sent to San Francisco to work until her last days on the water.

The T. J. Potter as she was originally built on the Columbia River around 1888. (Oregon Maritime Museum Collection)

The *T. J. Potter*, commonly referred to as the *Potter*, was probably the greatest sidewheeler to watch at that time, with its elaborate pierced side wheelhouses. When built, the *Potter* had a reputation as one of the fastest and most luxurious steamboats in the Pacific Northwest.

The *Potter* was named after Mr. T. J. Potter, First Vice President in charge of the Union Pacific Railroad operations in the west. He was joint manager of the Oregon Short Line and the Oregon Railway and Navigation Company, May 14, 1887, until his sudden death on March 9, 1888.

The *T. J. Potter* was built entirely of wood for the Oregon Railway and Navigation Company and was launched in Portland, Oregon, in 1888 by a firm owned by John F. Steffan. Every inch of her was refined elegance. Her paddle boxes were sophisticated; even her fan designs were jig sawed into an intricate floral pattern that made them look like works of Victorian art. A divided, curving staircase led up to the grand saloon, and her passengers could watch themselves in the biggest plate glass mirror on any West Coast steamer. Colored sunlight from the stained glass windows of the clerestory shone on silky carpeting and the rich wood and ivory of a grand piano.

Captain James W. Troup, one of the most famous steamboat captains, directed the construction of the *T. J. Potter*. Although most of her was built new, her upper cabins came from the steamboat *Wide West*. (These required alteration, because the *Potter* was a sidewheeler, whereas the *Wide West* had been a sternwheeler.)

The Wide West was christened and launched in Portland, August 15, 1877. She made her trial trip on October 17.   (Shaver Transportation Collection)

The *T. J. Potter* was 230 feet long, with a 33-foot beam, 659 gross tons, and a 10 ½-foot depth of hold. She was driven by two non-condensing steam engines, with 32-inch cylinders, each with an 8-foot stroke, and generating 1,700 horsepower. The Pusey & Jones Company, in Wilmington, Delaware, built her single boiler and firebox in 1887. The boiler was 32 feet long with a diameter of 84 inches. Her gross tonnage was 659 and her net tonnage was 589. She was placed on the seaside run soon after completion, in the charge of Captain Archie L. Pease, Pilot Edward Sullivan, and Chief Engineer Thomas Smith with assistant Phil Carnes, and Daniel O'Neil, purser.

Because of her distinguished speed, the O. R. & N. put the *T. J. Potter* on a tourist run from Portland to Astoria, taking less than six hours. Still, she had quite the competition from the *Telephone*, which could do the same run in 4 hours and 34 minutes. As the *Telephone* was more in demand, the *Potter* was moved up north to Puget Sound, Captain Pease, Engineer Smith, and Steward Charles Petrie going with her to compete with the *Bailey Gatzert*. Since the *Bailey Gatzert* was a sternwheeler, it did much better in the Sound than a sidewheeler. For the *Potter*, the waters there tossed her back and forth, raising one paddle out of the water then the other one. Even so, the *Potter* was one of the fastest steamboats on Puget Sound, and in 1890 beat the *Bailey Gatzert* in a race.

In March of 1895, the *T. J. Potter* again raced the *Bailey Gatzert* just a mile or so below the town of Cathlamet. The sternwheeler was going along with an easy speed with Cathlamet just a little more than a mile ahead. No one noticed the *Potter* sliding up behind her, just half a length behind under full steam to overtake her by surprise. Word was passed to the Chief Engineer Evans who threw the *Bailey Gatzert* open and then began a race for Cathlamet. The *Potter* had the advantage as the sternwheeler was under a low-pressure of steam and was handicapped by a restricted cutoff to her starboard engine, but she held her own. In addition, as both steamers approached the cannery wharf, the *Bailey Gatzert* pushed ahead, beating the *Potter* into Cathlamet by fully half a boat length. All folks in town had turned out to watch the race and the cheers that went up for the winner must have been heard across the water.

Finally, the *T. J. Potter* was transferred back to the Columbia River in 1889. She was placed on the Portland - Astoria run, where she competed with steamboats owned by other companies. The O. R. & N. struck a deal with Shaver Transportation where all of the Shaver boats would stay off the Portland - Astoria route in return for a monthly subsidy. She was placed back on Puget Sound again in 1890, participating in some lively steamboat races, and in June, she made a record of just 1 hour and 22 ½ minutes between Seattle and Tacoma. During her inland work, she raced the *City of Seattle*, *Bailey Gatzert*, and the *Multnomah*; she returned to the Columbia with a gilt greyhound and a broom on her pilothouse.

She made a round trip a day a on the Portland - Astoria route, alternating with the *R. R. Thompson*.

In 1901, the *T. J. Potter* was refurbished at a total cost of $86,000. By using the upper works, boiler and some machinery from the *Wide West*, they extended her length to 233.7 feet and her gross tons from 650 to 1,017 and her net tonnage from 590 to 826. Her width was now 35.6 feet, and depth 11.4. All of this gave her a big increase in her weight capacity, with the added bulk cutting several knots off her speed. The Willamette Iron Works cast new cylinders and she had the largest firebox of any steamboat on the Pacific Coast. Her wheelhouse was rebuilt, and instead of a flat roof, she had a blue dome with flagpole that was unique among Columbia River steamboats. The machinery was almost new and made her horsepower up to 2,100, whereas the old *Potter* could develop only 1200 horsepower. She was able to make two round trips on one supply of fire, so there was no delay in "wooding up."

An upper deck was added and the ceiling extended out to the roof of this new deck, which was set aside for her staterooms. There were 30 elegantly finished berths on the salon deck, and at the rear end of the main deck was the dining room, which seated up to 100 passengers. The women's salon was over 100 feet long and was both upholstered and carpeted in fusing shades of green. All the wood trimming was of a deep cherry stain. There were electric lights in every section and stateroom, which included at least 69 sleeping rooms. The *Potter* was more stunningly furnished than the *S. S. Olympian*; she was known as the "Floating Palace."

She was registered with customs on June 18, 1901, under the command of Captain J. L. Turner. The O. R. & N. then put her on the run from Portland to Ilwaco, Washington, to join with the narrow gauge Ilwaco Railway and Navigation Company, primarily to work the summer tourist trade. Captain Joe Turner ran her until another renovation in 1910, where she continued on the same run as before.

The passenger fares were $2.50 from Portland to Astoria, but this fluctuated with some discounts for a round trip; for one short period of time during an intense competition, passengers rode for as little as twenty-five cents. Lower berths were seventy-five cents and a single berth was fifty cents. A room was $1.25 added to the fare and all meals were fifty cents.

Sadly, in 1916 the *T. J. Potter* was condemned for passenger use and was never replaced. There was not enough passenger traffic to justify putting a new boat on the route, so she worked as a barracks boat for construction crews until her license was surrendered. She was abandoned on November 20, 1920. She was towed to Young's Bay, near Astoria, and believed to have later been stripped and burned for parts.

Steamboating above the Cascades had died down for a time until a group of entrepreneurs from The Dalles area decided they could run steamers for much less money than the Oregon Railway & Navigation Company was charging for freight and passengers. They named their company The Dalles - Portland Navigation Company (DPNC). In 1890, these men built an enormous storeroom in The Dalles, which expedited shipments of wheat and wool from the local farms to Portland. They built and bartered to have wharves on both sides of the Columbia River. Later, they added their own boats, the *Regulator* and *Dalles City*. Built in 1891, the *Regulator* was 152 feet long with a 28-foot beam. She was 434 gross tons with a 6-foot depth of hold, and her engines were 16 by 72 inches.

On July 13, 1898, while on her trip on the Columbia River, just below The Dalles, the *Regulator* wrecked on the rocks just below the Cascades. She had just crossed from Big Eddy to the lower entrance of the Cascades and was trying to enter the Government Locks when the winds picked up so strongly that she steered into the rapids. All 160 passengers, horses, and her freight were safely taken ashore. The boat sank up to her stateroom windows. She could not be raised, as the high winds would have torn her open.

The Regulator appears to be laid over and held by the current against a stone jetty.   (Oregon Maritime Museum Collection)

Also built in 1891, the *Dalles City* was 142 feet long, 26 feet wide and a 5-inch beam, with a 6-foot hold, and engines at 14 by 60 inches; she was later remodeled in 1909. She was one of four steamers, including the *Harvest Queen*, *Maria*, and the *Sarah Dixon* to go through the Cascade Locks when it opened on November 5, 1896.

The steamers were fitted for freight and passengers and recovered the river trade so well the O. R. & N. countered by building a new sternwheeler, the *Hassalo* in 1899 in Portland. (The third of this name: the first was spelled *Hassaloe*.)

The *Hassalo* was the first sternwheeler built in the Cascades, 181 feet long with a slim beam of 30 feet, 561 gross tons, and loaded she drew only 5 ½ feet. Her engines were horizontal, each with a high and low-pressure cylinder with a 98-inch stroke and 1,228 horsepower. She was constructed with the latest equipment, and she was easy to start as the two engines were operated by a single control. Her accessories were all of the latest fashion, especially the dining room, pantry, and kitchen; she looked like an elegant hotel on the water. She had a special three-toned steam whistle that gave the most melodic whistle on the river. When the *Hassalo* came in for a landing in Portland, people would stop and turn just to hear her blow.

Once the *Hassalo* was complete, her owners made test runs with her on the still water of Willamette Slough. They cheered when she swept off at twenty-six miles an hour, a pace great enough to let her run to Astoria in four hours. She proved to be the best boat on the river and ran regularly between Portland and Astoria.

Her biggest crowd was on October 4, 1880, when President Hayes, after attending summits in Vancouver, took a ride on the steamer the *Wide West* to The Dalles for meetings regarding the John Day River. Once those were finished, the President, along with officers from The Dalles city council boarded the *Hassalo*. She had been decorated with streamers, flowers, and colorful banners. Both sides of the river were filled with people waving and cheering her on as she guided the President through the scenic Cascades.

The *Hassalo* ran both the Astoria and Cascades routes, but her status came from the way she sped back and forth between The Dalles and Portland. She kept the *Telephone* and *T. J. Potter* busy protecting their standings against her claim to be the fastest riverboat. (A riverboat is a boat created for inland navigation on lakes, rivers, and manmade shipping canals. They are usually supplied and outfitted as workboats for freight or passenger transport, including tourism, such as lake or harbor tour boats. Built as a larger boat, nearly all riverboats are especially designed and constructed with features that enhance them as efficient service craft — such as dredgers, survey boats, fisheries management craft, fireboats and law enforcement patrol crafts.)

The steamboat Hassalo worked from 1880 to 1898 on the Columbia River and the Puget Sound, Washington. (Oregon Maritime Museum Collection)

She nearly proved this claim to be true in the summer of 1899 when she made a speed run which included no stops, no passengers or freight, between Astoria and Portland, making the 104 mile route in 4 hours, 22 3/4 minutes, with the current, and averaging somewhere around 23.7 mph. She made her return trip that same day, against the current, in only 6 hours. Her running time for the two-way trip was 10 hours, 22 3/4 minutes, averaging about 20 mph for the 208 miles.

Even with her speed, her luxury, and the many passengers that rode along for a tour, the Hassalo was slowly being ignored. Broken and finally left to rest along with many other sternwheelers, she was deserted in 1927. Her refined three-chimed whistle called "Old Faithful", stayed active long after the 20 some years it served on the Hassalo. It was relocated onto a new vessel on the Snake River, the Lewiston, built in 1923, for the Union Pacific's services picking up wheat along the Snake for delivery to U.P. trains at the town of Lewiston, Idaho. The Lewiston was sold in 1946 to Western Transportation Company in Portland, for use pushing barges between Crown-Willamette paper mills at West Linn, Camas and Portland docks and warehouses. The sternwheeler made a very bumpy passage down the Snake and Columbia Rivers to Portland, where the new owners changed her name to the Barry K, after the son of one of the Crown officials.

Barry K (ex-Lewiston of 1923), sternwheel steamer worked on the Willamette and Columbia Rivers from 1940 as a towboat for the Western Transportation Co. of Portland.
(Shaver Transportation Collection)

During World War II, the U. S. Army requisitioned the *Barry K*, whistle and all, for service on the Yukon and Tanana Rivers as a part of the Alaska Railroad operation. It was there that the *Barry K* ended her career after the war.

At the request of L. Rex Gault, the president of Western Transportation Company, the whistle was salvaged off the remains of the *Barry K* and returned to Portland. Gault had it placed on the company's sternwheeler steamer the *Claire*, which worked the *Barry K*'s former paper route. The *Claire* carried the whistle until the conclusion of an eventful excursion to Champoeg State Park where the Veteran Steamboatmen's Association (VSA) held its annual reunion in 1952. The passengers on the *Claire* were a mix of 200 members of the VSA and guests, including many retired steamboat captains and deckhands. The captains took turns pulling the whistle cord at every chance they could get.

When the *Claire* came to the Steel Bridge and Western's home moorage on the Willamette River, blowing for its last bridge opening, Rex Gault reached up and cut the whistle cord, a symbolic act meaning the end of her service. The *Claire* was stripped of her machinery and boiler and converted into a floating shop at the Western moorage. The whistle was subsequently stored, unused, on four different steamers. Then it had one last steamer to blow for; Gault gave the whistle to Homer T. Shaver, general manager of Shaver Transportation Company, to be mounted on the *Henderson*, and once again it delighted Portlanders with her musical sound. Sadly, after the *Henderson* was destroyed during a crash against a heavily loaded Liberty ship by big waves on December 9, 1956, the boat was declared a total loss. Back in Portland, a cold, freezing rain hit the whistle, ice froze in it, and its sides burst open. Shaver declared that the whistle could not be repaired and it was thrown away.

The Shaver Transportation Co. built the 160-foot sternwheeler, M.F. Henderson in 1901 as combination freighter and towboat. In 1911, during an overhaul, she lost the initials "M.F." and became the Henderson. The Henderson enjoyed a long and illustrious career on the Columbia towing log rafts, pushing barges, and tugging ships. By 1950, the Henderson was one of only two wood-hulled sternwheelers still working the river.

(Oregon Maritime Museum Collection)

THE STEAMERS *M. F. HENDERSON* AND *HENDERSON*

The *M.F. Henderson* was built at the Portland Shipbuilding Company in 1901 at the cost of $32,350. She was christened the *M. F. Henderson* after Mr. Milton F. Henderson, the Vice President and General Manager of the Eastern & Western Lumber Company. She was 158 feet 7 inches long with a 31-foot beam, and a 7-foot 1-inch depth of hold, and 534 gross tons. Her engines were 18 inches in diameter with an 84-inch stroke and were built by the Portland Iron Works. These engines were believed to be the first piston valve sternwheel engines ever made on the Columbia River with a rotary cutoff. The Portland Boiler Works managed by James Monk, one of the well-known Portland boilermakers, built her boiler.

The *M. F. Henderson* was the first limited freight and towing rig built for the Shaver Transportation Company. The previous steamers served as both freighter and passenger boats. She worked on the Clatskanie run to carry lumber, box shooks, and shingles from Clatskanie to Portland, usually towing one or more rafts on the same trip. On her return trip, she would haul canned goods, feed, and materials to the lower river and make stops at Rainier, Oak Point, Stella, and other harbors. With a crew of over a dozen men, insurance and general maintenance, her operating cost in 1902 was $64 a day for that entire year. In 1909, the freight business died down, so the *Henderson* was then used for moving rafts, logs, barges, and ships.

In 1911, while towing a Standard Oil barge from Astoria to Portland she collided at Bugby Hole with the steamer *Daniel Kern* which was pushing two loaded rock barges bound downriver to the Columbia River entrance jetties. The Columbia Contract Company owned the *Daniel Kern* from Portland, which was under contract to the U. S. Army Engineers to supply rock for the jetties. The *M. F. Henderson* sank, but as she rolled over, the crew was able to scramble up on her side. She turned over again and the crew crawled through the gangway and climbed up the other side. It was said that the steamer's cook crawled through the hawse pipe and was put aboard the Standard Oil barge. The *M. F. Henderson* lay on her side for several days. No lives were lost. The Shaver Transportation Company righted the wrecked boat by having five sternwheelers pulling at the same time. She was brought to the Portland Shipbuilding Company and then dismantled.

During an overhaul in 1912, she lost the initials "M.F." and became just the *Henderson*. The damaged hull was discarded and a new one of nearly the same dimensions was built by the shipyard. The original engines and machinery were installed in the new hull, and a new boiler, built by James Monk, could carry a fifty percent overload and would last the life of the boat without a cut in steam pressure. This new boiler cost $5,500 and the hull cost $15,500, making the total cost of reconstruction $35,000.

Much of the work steamers were used for was directing and guiding both ships and cargo through the water. Here is the M. F. Henderson and the Shaver pushing a cigar raft along the Columbia River. (Shaver Transportation Collection)

The new steamer was 159 feet in length, with a 31 ½-foot beam, and a 7-foot 1-inch depth of hold. She was Shaver's lead towboat and was kept very busy for 38 years until her second severe accident.

In 1929, the *Henderson* was upgraded again and equipped with tandem compound engines, with 15 by 84 inch high-pressure, and 26 by 84 inch low-pressure. This work was done by Sam Shaver of the machinist firm of Thayer, Shaver & Gulley, resulting in a net saving of 1 ½ barrels of fuel per hour while running. Some of the early captains on her crew were Jim Smith, the first master of the *M. F. Henderson*, Ezra "Hank" Berry, Henry Stayton, "Bob" Livingston, Linn Logan, Sydney J. "Happy" Harris, Harold Wolfe and Frank Hatcher. Other crew members over her early years were, Dan Conway as pilot, Jack Wendel, Second Engineer, Harry Lindley, Joe Hawkins, Chris O'Brien, and Hartley Morgan, who was in charge of the installation of the engines on the original *M. F. Henderson*, was her first Chief Engineer. The *Henderson* enjoyed a long and distinguished career on the Columbia towing log rafts, pushing barges, and tugging ships. In 1937, the U. S. Department of Commerce issue of *Merchant Vessels of the United States* reported that the *Henderson* was in passenger service with a crew of ten; even so, she rarely ever carried passengers. In 1948, she had new framing timbers and planking.

The *Henderson*'s second major accident was in 1949 when she lightly struck the Liberty ship *James W. Cannon* of the Coastwise Line while pushing into the Portland Locomotive dock (located on the west side of the Willamette near downtown Portland). This accident created a 20-foot long crack in the port side of the *Henderson*. The Albina Engine & Machine Works repaired the damage.

By 1950, the *Henderson* was one of only two wood-hulled sternwheelers still working the river. That same year, on Dec. 11, the *Henderson* and diesel tug *Chinook* were moving the decommissioned steamer *Pierre Victory* to layup in Astoria when a strong gust blew the whole tow very close to Cottonwood Island while it was making a turn southeast of Longview, Washington. The *Henderson* struck a submerged pile dike, causing a 20-foot rip in her hull. Captain Harris ordered the lines loosened from the *Pierre Victory*, which carried the towboat almost half a mile before they were separated. Don Weik, the pilot, beached the vessel at the sand spit off the Longview Fiber Company, near the mouth of the Cowlitz River and sank in the shallow water. The crew took to lifeboats, but came back when the sternwheeler came to rest with its main deck awash. The crew had breakfast on the second deck as if nothing had happened.

Meanwhile, Wilbur J. Smith's tugs of Rainer stood by the *Henderson*'s crew while the *Chinook* held the *Pierre Victory* in midstream, waiting for the arrival of the sternwheeler tug *Portland* to assist on the rest of the run to Astoria. The Shaver Transportation Company sent Fred Devine, diver, to the scene to assess what steps could be taken for getting the 38-year-old steamer to a repair yard.

The rip in the Henderson was repaired. She was able to return on her own to
Portland.   (Larry Barber Collection)

The *Henderson* was successfully refloated on December 13, the rip was
sealed, and she was pumped out and towed to Portland for permanent repairs.

Some of the scenes for the movie, Bend of the River, were filmed in Oregon with the steamer Henderson. (Larry Barber Collection)

In 1951, the movie *Bend of the River*, starring actors James Stewart, Arthur Kennedy, Rock Hudson, J. C. Flippen, Julia Adams, several other actors, plus about 50 local extras, was filmed in Oregon.

Some of the scenes were on the Columbia River using the sternwheeler *Henderson*, which the Shaver Transportation Company chartered to Universal - International Pictures of Hollywood. In the movie, the *Henderson* was outfitted and modified to represent a mid-1800s steamer called the *River Queen*.

To change its appearance for the filming, the towing winch on the forward deck, her official numbers from the bow and her big searchlights from the top of the pilothouse were all removed. Since the *Henderson* was made to look more like an old time river freighter than a sternwheel towboat, her fuel oil filter pipe on the forward deck was concealed with old canvas and coils of rope.

The *Henderson* was under the control of Captain Sydney J. "Happy" Harris and managed by her regular crew during the journey up the river to Rooster Rock's sandy beach for part of the filming. Shown as a deckhand when he was before the cameras, Captain Harris took the wheel and rang the bells when the ship was in motion.

The *River Queen* landed at a shallow beach along the Columbia Gorge, where the crew had constructed a wooden ramp to unload the wagons and horses. As the cameramen moved ashore, the actors performed their scene. "Jeremy," (played by J. C. Flippen) and his daughter in tears, said their goodbyes to "Captain Mello" (played by Chubby Johnson) and "Adam" (played by Stepin Fetchit) before the wagons continued their crossing over land to new homes.

Filmed in the summer of 1951, *Bend of the River* was ready for release by January of 1952. The city of Portland was chosen for the premiere on January 23. To get people energized about this film, a steamboat race on the Columbia River was staged between the old wooden hulled *Henderson* and the new steel hulled, four-year-old *Portland* sternwheelers. Captain Harris commanded the *Henderson* and Captain Bob Livingston the *Portland*.

The race course was a distance of 3 ½ miles; it was on the river from a red buoy 2,000 yards north of Reeder's Point on Sauvie Island to Light No. 40. This location was just downstream from the flowing together of the Willamette and Columbia Rivers. The race was run upstream against the afternoon current. The U. S. Coast Guard had many vessels assigned to patrol the raceway.

Gathered along the race course and near the finish line were about 100 private boats carrying several hundred spectators, including the movie actors. Actor Jimmy Stewart, his wife and J. C. Flippen, as well as photojournalists were guests on the cruiser *Nirvana*. Julia Adams, Lori Nelson, Susan Cabot, Rock Hudson, and many more photographers were on another boat. Both boats were anchored at the finish line. On the shores of Sauvie Island were thousands of people who had plodded through the marshlands to the dike parallel to the racecourse.

On January 23 around 12:30, the starting cannon, which was borrowed from the Portland Yacht Club, was fired from the boat, the *Behlma* and the race was on the move. The *Henderson* somehow lost her steam and the *Portland* immediately moved ahead. Charley Kern, the engineer got the *Henderson* under control by opening the bypass valves to send live steam directly to the compound engines installed in 1929. This increased the horsepower from 800 to about 1,100 and added considerable speed to the sternwheeler.

About halfway through the race the sternwheelers were running almost bow to bow, blowing black smoke mixed with white steam from their whistles. Both captains kept those whistles a blowing, which kept the crowds yelling and cheering for a winner. According to the press, Jimmy Stewart kept yelling and cheering for "his" boat, the *Henderson*.

The race between the Henderson and the Portland, in 1952, was one of the last steamboat races to occur on the Columbia River. (Larry Barber Collection)

Both crews knew the *Henderson* had an upper hand. She had a better hull, was lighter in weight and at full power she was more comfortable on the water than the rigid *Portland*.

As both sternwheelers approached the finish line, the old *Henderson* was putting out thirty turns a minute, an impressive rate for a tug designed for working, not racing. The forty-year-old wooden hulled *Henderson* kept pushing on ahead. Even though a safety valve popped, she held her own and won the race. A number of skeptics claimed it was planned that way, but the movie crew had no comment.

The time of the race was 19 minutes and the *Henderson*'s average speed was logged at 11.3 knots, or 13.2 miles per hour. Unfortunately, only seconds later three fusible plugs popped on the *Henderson*, releasing the steam pressure. She was dead in the water and had to be towed back to her berth at Shaver's by the diesel tug *James W.*

On December 9, 1956, while pushing the loaded Liberty ship *John M. Schofield* out of the Maritime Administration's Astoria Reserve Fleet basin near Tongue Point, the *Henderson* had her last and fatal accident. Strong southeast winds, estimated at 40 knots, had whipped up 6 to 8 feet heavy swells against a flood tide near the mouth of the Columbia, which caused the *Schofield* and the *Henderson* to both roll violently against each other. The *Henderson*'s house and hull were crushed and the main boiler knocked out of position.

Captain Hatcher and his crew got her away from the *Schofield* and started pumps to keep her afloat. Shaver's tug the *Chinook* and two Maritime tugs were unable to handle the ship so the powerful *Salvage Chief*, owned by Fred Devine, was called upon to tow it to Longview to discharge 6,000 tons of wheat stored in her hull. The *Schofield* was one of several idle ships used for storing surplus grain at a time when commercial elevators were full. The *Chinook* went back to the *Henderson* and assisted in her to return to Portland. In drydock, the shattered sternwheeler was surveyed by an insurance company and declared a "constructive total loss." She was retired on January 9, 1957. She was the last wooden hulled steam sternwheeler on the Columbia River system, having served for 55 years, except for two or three years when she was laid up for heavy repairs.

The *Henderson* was put up for sale and was purchased by Loren and Howard Anderson of Columbia City, where she was beached on the new owner's property for use as a shop and office for their boat moorage. The boiler was still in working condition and was sold to a South American company. After that, the *Henderson* languished on the shore until she was burned to salvage scrap metal in 1964.

The Henderson travels on one of her last trips on the Columbia River.
(Oregon Maritime Museum Collection)

THE STEAMBOAT *GEORGIANA*

As trains and highways were moving into the Northwest Territory, the rivers were still active with steamers transporting both people and cargo between the shores. Over time, both the quickness and comfort of a train was attracting more customers than the boats. Seeing this change in transportation, some steamboat companies created their own links with the railroads and the bodies of water where they ran their crafts, including one of the smaller screw propelled steamboats on the lower Columbia River, the *Georgiana*. She was built of wood and constructed for the Harkins Transportation Company, which was founded in 1914, and ran steamboats all along the lower Columbia River until they went bankrupt in 1937.

The *Georgiana* was built at Joseph Supply's yard in Portland, Oregon. She was named in honor of three well-known women, Georgiana, the wife of Henry L. Pittock, and her granddaughters, Georgiana Leadbetter and Georgiana Gantenbein. Lyle Owen Hosford was the first captain of the *Georgiana*, and his sister Cora christened the vessel at her launching on June 20, 1914.

The Harkins Transportation Company wanted her for carrying both passengers and a minimum amount of freight. The *Georgiana* was considered a "day boat" on which passengers were urged to carry their own lunch. Her dollar fare on the 105 mile run between Portland and Astoria was meant to attract those who could not afford the higher ticket prices of a train trip.

She was small, only 261 tons, 135 feet long with a 22 ½-foot beam, compared to some of the other boats that ran on the river such as the *T. J. Potter*, and the beautifully refurbished *Bailey Gatzert*. The *Oregonian* newspaper had compared the *Georgiana* to a yacht. Her main lounge and smoking rooms were very clean and pleasant and her Pullman-type seats were built next to large windows to let passengers enjoy the scenery without feeling cramped.

The *Georgiana* shuttled on the Columbia River, making Washington landings on the downriver morning runs and Oregon stops on the afternoon return. Her competitor, the127-foot in length screw propelled steamer, the *Astorian* (formerly the 1911 Olympia - Tacoma steamer the *Nisqually* of Puget Sound) owned by the Oregon Railway & Navigation Company (ORNC) was a similarly designed boat that had been brought down to the Columbia River in 1918.

Finally, one spring day in April of 1920, the steamers gave the public one of the last genuine and unofficial steamboat races on the Columbia River. As the smoke spiraled from their stacks, they raced each other the entire 110 miles from Portland to Astoria. The *Georgiana* made five scheduled stops, and the *Astorian* only two, yet the *Georgiana* won, beating her rival by 5 hours and 45 minutes berth to berth, and exceeding her by three distant miles. That afternoon the *Astorian* evened the score on the 110-mile return and the *Georgiana's* supporters cried "Foul!" Their boat had made nine scheduled stops to the *Astorian's* two at Skamokawa and Cathlamet, but the *Georgiana* had to stop and fuel up in Linnton.

While running at full speed in 1921, the *Astorian* broke her shaft, suffering major damage, which took her out of service until she was returned to Puget Sound. This left *Georgiana* and the other Harkins Transportation Company boats (*Undine*, *Lurline*, and *Madeline* {formerly the *Joseph Kellogg*}) as the only working steamboats on the Columbia River. In an effort to keep their business going, the ORNC put the *Iralda*, a lighter steam propeller, on the Astoria run in 1921, but it couldn't match the *Georgiana*.

Built in Portland for W. S. Newsom, the Iralda was ninety feet long, thirteen feet beam, feet six inches hold, with engines eight, thirteen and twenty by twelve inches; she was a very fast steamer. (Larry Barber Collection)

After the Harkins Transportation Company filed bankruptcy in 1937, a Portland businessman, Ralph J. Staehli, bought the *Georgiana*. She stayed on the lower river until 1939; she was a loss since her earnings had fallen dramatically with the new railroad system. She had spent over 25 years working on the rivers. Her captain from 1918 - 1932, John L. Starr, had logged over 650,000 miles on board.

With the new Bonneville Dam in place, and the rolling Columbia River filled into a lake, Staehli kept her working for another year. He polished her up with a new coat of white paint and renamed her *Lake Bonneville*. He put her on the Portland - Bonneville Dam tour run, but it was a lost cause. The second World War ended the excursion trade, and there just was not enough work, so the beautiful old boat was sent to retirement. Finally, she was beached on Sauvie Island, within sight of the channel she had driven countless times, until the hull slowly rolled over and settled into the sands.

In 1904, a group of businessmen from Portland created the Open River Navigation Company. Their goal was to compete with the railroad that had taken over carrying wheat from The Dalles down to Portland. They used the sternwheeler *Mountain Gem*, built in Lewiston for operation above Celilo and they had four more steamers that carried sacked grain from the upper river to the Cascades where it was transferred to the lower riverboats running to Portland. One of their goals was to get the government's interest in building the proposed Celilo Canal and locks. Since the railroads continued to haul grain, the Open River Company was forced to sell out to Captain F. B. Jones, owner of The Dalles - Portland River Line Company. Captain Jones tried to run the steamers, *Twin Cities* and *State of Washington*, but he, too, had to shut his business down. Shortly after this, the Regulator Line and the Peoples' Transportation Company kept their run as far as The Dalles with intermediate stops, but they, too, had to shut down.

Before the construction of locks was built past the Cascade Rapids, passengers and cargo would travel the lower Columbia River to the Cascades on the *Fashion, Carrie Ladd, Mountain Buck*, or *Julia*. There they would go on shore and ride the portage railroad behind a tiny rail car, called the *Oregon Pony* to the upper landing; there they would embark the *Idaho, Hassalo*, or *Wasco* to The Dalles. Once they arrived there they would use a horse drawn wagon for a short ride around the falls then board the *Colonel Wright, Nez Perce Chief, Yakima*, or *Spray* for a journey to Lewiston on the Snake River. This practice continued until a canal similar to the one built at Cascade Locks was finished.

By 1900, the new plan for a canal was ready. It called for two locks and a 3000-foot canal around Celilo Falls, a 33-foot lift lock, a 9000-foot canal around Fivemile Rapids, with a submerged dam at the head of these rapids, and the development of navigational maps at Threemile Rapids. The whole project was to cost four million dollars.

In May of 1903, a hearing in Portland modified the plans to provide for a continuous canal with four locks from Big Eddy to the head of Celilo Falls. On June 13, 1902, Congress approved the project. The Secretary of the Army gave his endorsement on the canal project in November. A month later, the Oregon State legislature estimated one hundred thousand dollars to purchase right of way for the canal. The State set aside four hundred and seventy-nine acres to the United States in April of 1905.

The U.S. Army Corps of Engineers designed a canal and lock system to get around the most winding turns of the Columbia River. It took nearly 12 years to build a channel and locks around the water barriers between The Dalles and Celilo in 1915, opening river navigation between the ocean and Lewiston, Idaho - a distance of 465 miles. It was called the Celilo Canal and was 65 feet wide, 8 miles long and 8 feet deep with periodic turnouts to allow boats to pass each other. Today it is underwater, behind The Dalles Dam.

To honor the completion of the canal on May 15, 1915, a celebration attracted over 25,000 people to the "Open Road to the Sea." The steamers *J. N. Teal*, *Inland Empire*, and *Undine* carried dignitaries and paying guests to celebrate a new era for the river. The *J. N. Teal*, commanded by Captain Arthur Riggs, continued on to Lewiston to emphasize this new canal. One hundred guns saluted the river as the sun rose and did so again at sunset that day. In 1918, the entrance channel of the Columbia River was dredged to a depth of 40 feet to allow larger vessels to enter the estuary.

Sternwheelers continued plodding on, hauling passengers and grain along The Dalles - Portland run, but with much less demand. In 1930, when the steamer *Cowlitz* was put to work hauling wheat out of The Dalles, she was caught by a 25 mph wind. She had a heavy load and huge swells flooded the engine room. Captain Exton tried to turn her around to dock but the swells overran the boat and it sank.

Two years later, a former Arizona mule team driver and trucker, Lew. S. Russell, who worked for Leland James, head of Consolidated Truck Lines of Portland, suggested to Mr. James that the steamers could be used for the long haul with trucks working as feeders at both ends. This idea worked for a while along the Columbia River but the railroads kept taking their business.

The J. N. Teal along the downstream entrance at Big Eddy, Oregon, which was located on the mid-Columbia River near Celilo Rapids.

(Oregon Maritime Museum Collection)

The next step for these two men, along with Captain Shaver, was to create the Shaver Forwarding Company to use many of their aging sternwheelers. They ran these steamers in The Dalles and Umatilla, carrying general freight and oil and brought back sacked wheat and fresh farm produce. The business began well, but then the 34-year old *Hercules* wrecked at Threemile Rapids and the *Beaver* struck the rocks at Canoe Encampment Rapids. The *Undine* was fitted with oil tanks and renamed *The Dalles* to become the first commercial petroleum carrier on the river. Russell had to buy oil in Portland and then sell it upcountry. The oil companies had little confidence in this venture after the steamers wrecked.

For a while, *The Dalles* carried apples and pears from Hood River, Oregon, and White Salmon, Washington, for delivery to a cold storage plant at Portland's Terminal 4. Then they packed new automobiles back up to Hood River. They would also load up Pabst Beer (shipped out by rail from Milwaukie to Portland) destined for Hood River and The Dalles, which were both along the railroad lines.

They shipped soap and other general cargo that had come up from California on a through rate agreement with Hammond Steamship Company. Business struggled against the fast and efficient railroad, so in 1940, the company merged with Tidewater Transportation Company, forming the Tidewater - Shaver Barge Lines.

The Hosford Transportation Company tried to get into the upper river trading, but they couldn't compete with the railroads. It had the steamer *Weown* working along the Cascade Rapids and delivering goods all along that area.

The sternwheeler Weown was built in Portland in 1907 by the St. Johns Shipbuilding Company yards for the Columbia and Cowlitz River Transportation Co. (Larry Barber Collection)

A newcomer to the Cascades was Kirk Thompson, who distributed oil throughout eastern Washington. He created his own shipping line, the Tidewater Transportation Company, and used the 56-foot diesel tug *Mary Gail,* and a 100,000-gallon oil barge, which he had built up in Seattle. Thompson modernized this type of river transportation that is still seen today.

The U.S. steamboating era lasted into the late 1940s on the Columbia River and into the 1950s in British Columbia. Portland continued to progress and with the ongoing increase of business and home development, transportation needs changed. As the canals altered the formation of the rivers, so did the newly built dams, such as the Bonneville, The Dalles, McNary and John Day on the Columbia River, and four more dams on the Snake River. Soon the graceful steamboats would be docked as the new diesel tugs came into play; they were much more efficient and less expensive to run. Steamboats slowly sat aside to barges, railroads and trucks, which could move larger amounts of cargo and people faster and at lower cost. Today, of the more than 500 steamers that worked the waters of the Columbia, Willamette and Snake Rivers and their tributaries during the past hundred years, only the sternwheeler *Portland* remains on the water as a reminder of a long forgotten time.

The Portland is traveling along the Columbia River.

(Capt. Dale Russell Collection)

THE FIRST *PORTLAND* STEAMERS

A sidewheeler built in Westport, Oregon, was called the *Portland No. 1*. She was a ferryboat 101 feet in length and 107 gross tons. Little is known about this first *Portland* sternwheeler, but she was disposed of in 1880.

The next *Portland* steamer was a small 90-foot sidewheeler, launched July 2, 1853. Alexander S. Murray and Jack Torrance built this sidewheeler to run between Oregon City and Portland. Murray, Torrance, and Captain Archibald Jamieson owned this *Portland*.

In 1853, Captain George W. Hoyt and Captain Murray created the People's Line using a few steamers for their business. This was one of the first mergers of steamboats on the Willamette River. The *Portland*'s typical day in 1853 would begin at 9 a.m. in Oregon City for her Portland route. She would leave Portland at 2 p.m. to return to Oregon City. After a while, the *Portland*'s course increased. She then went from Oregon City up to the Upper Willamette River to and from Portland and Vancouver, along with the sidewheeler *Multnomah*.

Three years later, Capt. Murray took his *Portland* steamer and joined with Captain Jamieson to make a new service, the Citizen's Line. This increased the steamer's routes and times.

Captain Murray had been running the *Portland* in connection with the *Enterprise*, but took her off the route in September to make a few trips to Astoria, replacing the *Multnomah*, which was laid up for maintenance. She continued on this course until October of 1856, preempted by the return of the *Multnomah*, under the command of Captain Jamieson. Her next tour took her above the falls, running the Upper Willamette River until March of 1857.

One of the most tragic maritime casualties of 1857 was that of the steamer *Portland*. She was swept over the falls at Oregon City, around 5 p.m. on March 17, St. Patrick's Day, drowning two men. The sidewheeler had left the town of Canemah under the command of Captain Jamieson, who intended to take her into the basin at Oregon City to drop off some cargo. The engineer, a brother of the captain, remained onshore, so the only other persons on board were firefighter, Peter Anderson, and a deckhand named Alexander Bell. While entering the basin, the *Portland* wandered in too far and because the river was unusually high, the current caught her. Before the men knew of it, she eased toward the rim of the basin. Once the captain knew the hazardous position in which they were in, he ordered the men to get the vessel under control, but the boilers didn't have enough steam and she could make no headway against the current.

On the bank, Captain George Pease saw the boat struggling with the current. Realizing the danger, he threw out lines and called to the men to jump overboard and grab them. Anderson immediately dived into the water, grabbed a rope, and was hauled in safely by Captain Pease. Captain Jamieson and Bell hesitated for a moment, jumped in too late, and were quickly pulled to their deaths. (If Captain Jamieson and Bell had stayed on board their lives might have been saved.)

The *Portland* went over the falls stern first. When it landed below the rapids, the house and upper works dropped off and went on down river, coming ashore in the city of Portland relatively intact. The steam whistle cracked off just as the steamer broke in half. The pilothouse was picked up by a steamer near the mouth of the Willamette. Sadly, the *Portland* was a complete wreck.

The sternwheeler *Jennie Clark* was coming upriver, heading for Oregon City. Pieces of the *Portland* were floating by. The crew was able to salvage some of the wreckage, recovering some mattresses, blankets, a trunk, a carpet bag, and the steamer's whistle and compass. Another section of the *Portland* floated a few miles downstream and was found by a man on shore. He searched through the shattered upper deck and found $75. The mattresses in the cabin room were still dry. At the time of the wreck, the *Portland* had been valued at $8,000. No plans were made then to recover its machinery. (Because of other maritime tragedies, the deaths of the Jamieson brothers, including the wreck of the *Portland*, were the subject of a 1999 song, *The Steamboatin' Jamiesons*, performed by the Canadian musical group, Tiller's Folly.)

The next Portland was the first sternwheeler built in Portland.
(Oregon Maritime Museum Collection)

The following *Portland* was a steamer sternwheeler built in 1919 that started working right after World War I. The Port of Portland owned her, and used her as a towboat for docking and moving vessels within the Portland Harbor. She was invaluable for helping move deep draft ships through the Willamette River bridges during times of strong currents up to 5 mph and winds of 40 to 50 mph. It was a common sight to see her on the Columbia River assisting oceangoing ships in docking, undocking, and moving the ships in the narrow turning basin. With her ability to pilot and refloat stranded vessels, she was on call 24 hours a day.

This *Portland* was built with speed and proficiency in mind. She was one of the largest and most powerful wooden hull sternwheelers of her kind and was 185 feet long at 801 gross tons. Her build was long and narrow with a short cabin resting on top of the freight deck. The Texas and pilothouse were at the bow. Her uncovered sternwheel was uncommon on the river during that time.

Here is the Portland in 1937, shown on the left and the sternwheeler, the Umatilla on the right. They are towing a half-sunken Italian freighter, the Feltre. They are taking this ship to the Portland dry docks. (Larry Barber Collection)

ABOARD THE *PORTLAND (II)*

The *Portland*, built in 1919, was ready to be retired. She had been on the water for nearly 30 years and the necessary repairs for her could cost as much or more than replacing her with a new vessel. The Port of Portland Commission called a meeting on January 23, 1946, to get knowledgeable opinions from ship builders and operators. During this discussion, L. R. Hussa, president of the Albina Engine & Machine Works, led several representatives who advocated for building a twin screw tug, with two 500-horsepower General Motors diesel engines, and Kort nozzles for propulsion. (The Kort nozzles would be around the propellers, directing the flow of water, a method found highly successful on the Mississippi River system.) Diesel engines, they argued, did not require 24-hour attention and they stopped and started with the turn of a key. Fewer crew staff were needed as it only took the Captain with the key and a deckhand to run the electrical winches. This new boat, Hussa affirmed, would be an up-to-date boat, very navigable and economical.

In contrast, many of the Portland harbor pilots insisted that a powerful sternwheel of large size and conventional design was perfectly suited for maneuvering ocean vessels in the narrow confines of the Willamette River. Captain Shaver ran the controversy in favor of a ship-assist sternwheeler with steam power. Even though the design Hussa proposed was better for running the barges on the upper Columbia, these men felt a sternwheeler would be more practical for moving deep draft ships through the bridges with strong winds and currents. After this heated discussion, some of the fellows of the nine-member commission changed their views from a propeller boat to a sternwheeler.

Another meeting was held one month later with the port commissioners and the river pilots. Captain Clyde Raabe of the Columbia River Pilots made the point that a sternwheeler would have more power, steering, reversing and side-to-side handling than a propeller boat. He related many examples, such as in a quick flow from the river, five knots or better, the water can pile up two feet on the upstream face of bridge abutments, which could push a tug off course. Turning any vessel in this water, he told the commissioners, requires the maneuverability and the immediate throttle response only steam can produce.

They considered sending representatives to the East Coast to study how diesel tugs fared in their waters. The plan was turned down since no harbors there could be found with bridges, tides, and winds like those in Portland. After an extensive dispute, the pilots won and the new *Portland* was to be built.

Marine architect Guy H. Thayer, port commissioner chief engineer James Healey, and W. C. Nickum & Sons drew up plans for a steam-powered, steel-hulled sternwheel ship-assist tug. Requests for bids went out on August 25.

Albina Engine & Machine Works, Inc. submitted a bid of $522,382 and estimated 10 months until completion. Other bids came from the Kaiser Company and L. S. Baier. Even though the sum was much more than the Port of Portland wanted to spend, the Northwest Marine Ironworks, Inc. won with its low bid of $472,000, and projected completion of a mere 200 days. Much of the needed steel forms would be constructed in their shops, while final assembly would be completed at the Gunderson Brothers shipyard.

The Portland's keel was set on February 3, 1947, at the Gunderson Brothers Engineering Corporation's dry dock. (Larry Barber Collection)

The building of the house was comparable in general form and design to the houses of past sternwheelers still working on the waters. The sides of the house were made of steel to the first deck and marine plywood was used for the upper decks. The main deck was wider than other boats, so the crew could run lines without interference from the house sides; this gave the pilot better visibility. Above the main deck was a welded steel deckhouse. She also had a two-tier wood tongue and groove frame housing the cabins, fitted toward the bow by the wheel house and adjoining boiler stack.

When she was completed, the *Portland* was 219 feet (overall), gross tonnage of 928 tons, with a 42-foot beam, drew 5 ½ feet fully loaded, a shallow draft of 7 feet, a capacity for 133 tons of fuel, 80 tons of feed water and 2 tons of potable water. She had three decks, two Babcock & Wilcox oil-fired boilers, twin engines made to produce 900-horse power steam, and a 25 feet diameter paddle wheel made of Douglas fir. (Two 900 horsepower single expansion, non-condensing Babcock & Wilcox water tube boilers supply the energy that drives the port and starboard pitman rods.) She was 26 feet wide, with 20 rows of paddles, or buckets, and seven rudders. Her 186-foot steel hull was butt welded to make her the most navigable steam sternwheeler to work on the local rivers. The wooden paddlewheel was propelled by two horizontal high-pressure single cylinder noncondensing expansion steam engines designed by Sam H. Shaver.

The original Portland steamer had one last job to perform. She towed the new Portland, on May 24, 1947, to the Port of Portland's dry dock to be completed.
(Larry Barber Collection)

On May 24, 1947, the *Portland* was unveiled on the Willamette River and Mrs. William Zavin, daughter of Joseph Grebe, president of the Northwest Marine Iron works, set her off along with her sister, Mrs. Ray Terson as the matron of honor. The Rev. Ray Dunn, pastor of the Rose City Methodist Church in Portland, gave a spiritual blessing for the new craft and her crew. Mayor Earl Riley was the master of ceremonies and led the way for the *Portland*'s launching.

She did not disappoint anyone as she sped through the harbor, escape valves quietly chuffing, a rainbow-like shade of spray soaring back from the paddlewheel, and a plume of white steam curling from the tall black stack.

Official trials were held on August 23, 1947, when the *Portland* made a four-hour run in the lower harbor and in the Columbia River. The *Portland's* length gave her a critical advantage when shifting ships against the current; her powerful sternwheel bit deeply for thrust in pushing or backing out of the water. Four main rudders and three monkey rudders, that clever Colombia River invention, provided agility so the *Portland* literally could move sideways. The river pilots were all quite satisfied. Now the new *Portland* was ready for towing big ships on both the Columbia and Willamette Rivers to and from Vancouver, Washington, and other river ports, such as those in Astoria.

On August 29, the Northwest Marine Iron Works delivered her to the Port of Portland and the Shaver Transportation Company then managed her under an agency agreement at first. The main job for this assist tug was to support oceangoing ships in the Columbia River system by docking, undocking, directing them in the narrow turning basin, and passing through Portland's many bridge spans, of which there were nine in the post War period and eleven today. For the *Portland*, piloting and refloating marooned watercrafts was a 24-hour operation needing a crew of fifteen, split into two watches, which included a captain, pilot, two mates, two engineers, two firemen, six deckhands and a cook: her boilers never ran cold.

The Shaver Company lost the *Portland* in 1968 to Willamette Tug and Barge Company, although she still carried the stack markings of Shaver Transportation Company of the past 20 years. Now stationed across the Willamette River, she worked ships in and out of the dock at the Louis Dreyfus grain elevator at the east end of the Steel Bridge.

The *Portland* seldom left the harbor owing to a policy of the port commission to keep her close to home for the accessibility of the steamship people. One time she went to Astoria to tow a broken ship to Longview when no other tug capable of the job was available. Twice she was sent up the Columbia River on social missions. The *Portland* went to Pasco, Washington, in June of 1972 to emphasize to the people of Inland Empire that the city of Portland was their exporting port and to let them know how much the town appreciated their business.

The Portland is passing through The Dalles Lock and Dam, Oregon, on the Columbia River in 1972.   (Larry Barber Collection)

In June of 1975, she traveled 340 miles to Lewiston, Idaho. While there, she participated in celebrating completion of eight new dams in the Columbia and Snake Rivers system with projects that opened a watery highway to bring down grain and other goods of the inland.

Several days a year the U. S. Coast Guard permitted the *Portland* to carry passengers for special events, including a harbor cruise once a year for newly hired Portland Public school teachers to see the harbor directly from the water. Other times the sternwheeler would take community groups or visiting guests out for a historical tour. These tours were prized by the both the Port of Portland and eager travelers. She even had a Hollywood role in a 1966 movie filmed in Oregon: *The Last Trumpet*, the story of General George Armstrong Custer's last stand.

For the next 34 years, this *Portland* dependably worked up and down the Willamette River towing ships, helping them into and out of berths, and through the bridges, sometimes responding to calls several times a day. She even rescued ships trapped on sandbars.

In 1952, the heavy-laden *S. G. Follis,* an inbound tanker, ran aground in the Columbia River near the mouth of the Willamette River. The tanker lost her steering and by the time she was stopped, her bow was deep into the sandy bottom at the Sauvie Island dike, approximately ten miles northwest of downtown Portland. Many tugs tried to free her, but she remained until the *Portland* came to her rescue. When she arrived on the scene, she put lines aboard the stranded ship and began her work. With *Portland's* powerful engines in reverse, the wash from her paddle wheel began to loosen the sand under the tanker. Her rudders were able to work the ship from side to side until the force underneath was broken and the ship moved backward, free from the sand and the river bottom. Once she was afloat, the *Portland* helped tow her into Portland and dock her.

As she was coming in to Portland in 1952, an inbound tanker, the R. G. Follis, ran aground in the Columbia River near the mouth of the Willamette River. She was loaded with freight. Several tugs tried to free her, but it was left to the maneuverability of the Portland sternwheeler to free her. (Larry Barber Collection)

On Sunday, April 14, 1957, two vessels, which were set to be scrapped for their metal, were tied to the salvagers' dock in the Willamette River upstream from the Hawthorne Bridge, one of the main avenues from eastside to the downtown businesses in Portland. Unexpectedly, a huge gale force wind stormed into the city. *Chateau Thierry*, a retired army transport ship, and the decommissioned hospital liner *Louis A Milne*, were tied together and both broke free. The wind tore both vessels from their mooring and pushed them downstream, where they crashed sideways into the Hawthorne Bridge, just missing the lift span. Pressure from the wind on the Hawthorne was enormous. Two of the strongest diesel tugs in the area were called on for this catastrophe. Neither the *Peter W* nor the *George Birney* could move either stranded ship. All they could do was ease the strain from the bridge.

Soon Captain Jack Taylor brought the *Portland* steaming up from downriver. He put her lines aboard the *Chateau Thierry* and quickly had her moving away from the bridge. The *Portland* took the ship just upstream to a lumber company dock. Once she was secured, the *Portland* returned to the bridge and removed the *Louis A Milne* in the same manner. With her speedy service, the *Portland* prevented the strain from these battered ships breaking the Hawthorne Bridge. The Columbia River Pilots Association saw this incident as justification for having insisted that the *Portland* be a steam-powered sternwheeler.

(The Columbia River Pilots Association oversees the safe passage of all oceangoing ships on the Columbia and Willamette Rivers. To do this, a pilot boards a ship when it both enters and exits the Columbia River system. The pilot stays on board until it is safely moored or when a ship is in port, has left the area. These pilots have studied for and passed a strict U.S. Coast Guard examination; they have spent years on the rivers and know of all the navigational hazards.)

During the 1940s and 1950s, the U.S. Army Corps of Engineers created developmental plans for dams in the Columbia and Snake River basins. One of the advantages from these dams included providing a waterway for barge traffic to reach the town of Lewiston and grain growing areas in the inland Northwest. Construction of the Ice Harbor Dam on the Lower Snake River began in 1957. Lower Monumental and Little Goose Dams were built on the Lower Snake River in the 1960s. Lower Granite Dam was the last dam on the Lower Snake River; it provided a reservoir with slack tide so Lewiston would be accessible to barge traffic. Other benefits of these dams promised by the Corps were both flood control and hydropower production.

Congress provided initial building funds for the Lower Granite project in 1965. Unfortunately, this was also at the height of the Vietnam War, so general construction was slowed to a halt for several years.

In 1970, the Association of Northwest Steelheaders sued the Corps of Engineers. They wanted to stop the building of Lower Granite Dam, and to stop another planned dam for the Snake River near Asotin. The Association claimed that the project would affect salmon and steelhead runs, and that the Corps didn't meet the stipulations of the National Environmental Policy Act (NEPA) and the Fish and Wildlife Coordination Act. The State of Washington joined in on the lawsuit.

In spite of the lawsuit, the Corps continued creating the Lower Granite Dam. When the district court dismissed the case in December of 1971, the dam was already halfway completed.

Both the Steelheaders and the State of Washington took the case to the U.S. Court of Appeals. In 1973, that court reversed the lower court's decision, and advocated reinstatement of the lawsuit. In the meantime, the Corps continued building the Lower Granite Dam. Finally, in 1977, the U.S. District Judge ruled mainly in favor of the Corps because the matter had become unsettled since by that time all four dams on the Lower Snake River, including Lower Granite Dam, were completed and in operation. The judge ruled that the Corps had failed to study and report on fish and wildlife resources and ordered the Corps to file a report describing plans to enhance fish runs and the Corps complied.

Because the Corps' continued construction all during the lawsuit proved to be effective, the slack water reached Lewiston in February of 1975, and Lower Granite generated its first electricity in April of 1975. With the completion of the Lower Monumental, Little Goose, and Lower Granite Dams, and their navigational locks, they provided a 465-mile inland seaway through the Cascade Mountains to Lewiston; this was the farthest inland waterway available in Western America.

In June of 1975, the *Portland*, overseen by Captain Taylor, steamed all the way upriver, some 310 miles from Portland, Oregon, to Lewiston, Idaho, to help celebrate completion of the system of dams that have made the Columbia/Snake inland waterway a highway of rich commerce leading to Portland's grain elevators, the Port's Terminal 6 container complex, and then on to the markets of the world. She led a convoy of government, commercial and private crafts upstream on the river to dedicate these dams.

In December of 1974, the *Portland* assisted towing the fractured ship *Dianna* from Astoria to Longview, Washington; this was the largest tow of her career. She got the job because of the absence of another tug of similar size.

She was often seen by people watching along the shore of the Columbia River while she worked ships in and out of the dock at the end of the Louis Dreyfus grain elevator at the east end of the Steel Bridge in Portland.

The *Portland*'s most significant ship assist came on February 18, 1980, when she helped the Chinese flagged ship *Rong Cheng* dock at the Port of Portland's Terminal 4. This was the first Chinese ship to bring cargo to the U.S. in 30 years and signified the city of Portland as her first port of call.

PROFILES OF TWO *PORTLAND* CAPTAINS

Captain Dale Russell:

(Capt. Dale Russell Collection)

Captain Russell's maritime life had been spent well on the Portland rivers. He started working in electrical line construction for the Russell (no relationship) Towboat and Moorage (which later became the Tidewater Barge Lines in 1947.) The Russell Company broke him into working on the tugboats. Dale transferred his skills to work as a crewman for the Western Tug and Barge Co.

During World War II, Dale joined the Coast Guard and spent 2 years overseas. While he was stationed in the northwest, he worked in the shipyards. He kept building his maritime skills on each new assignment. After the war, he studied and soon became a licensed captain and ran little barges for the Camas Mill in Washington.

Captain Russell worked for Willamette Tug & Barge Company, Shaver Transportation Company, Umpqua River Navigation Company, the Kaiser Shipyards and Western Tug and Barge again. He mostly managed the tugboats, such as the *Invader*. Before long Captain Russell was learning how to handle steam tugs with his first sternwheeler the *Jean* that he ran along the Willamette River.

The Jean was one of Captain Russell's favorite boats.
(Capt. Dale Russell Collection)

One of Captain Russell's unforgettable jobs was with the Umpqua Company along the rivers hauling shale rock on his boat then using cranes for unloading them. Some of these rocks were the size of a small car. His most challenging work was maneuvering the steamboats for Schnitzer Steel in Portland, Oregon, in their narrow harbor. However, one of his most exciting jobs was hauling some 4,000 projectiles that were spilled along the Columbia River.

On September 24, 1953, a tug leased by Tidewater Barge Lines, the *Columbia Queen*, was pushing the barge *Racquette* on the Columbia River. It was rammed into by the *Hawaiin Planter*, owned by the Matson Navigation Company, which was also cruising along the Columbia off Brookfield, Washington. Powered by a 600 horsepower diesel engine, the *Columbia Queen* was a wooden tugboat with a hull of 81.1 feet in length, 21.3 feet in beam. The *Racquette* was an unmanned steel barge, without her own power; she was 189.7 feet long with a beam of 34 feet.

When the accident occurred, the tug was maneuvering the barge filled with 700 tons of 8-inch artillery shells from Bangor, Washington, to the Umatilla, Oregon, Ordnance Depot on the upper Columbia River. These projectiles were not fused, but still had to be safely recovered from the river. Captain Russell and Morris Devine (a well-known diver and salvager from Portland) created hooks to catch the rings on each sunken shell that they found. The stress for these men and their crew was hoping that none of the sunken ammunition was an explosive device.

Captain Russell worked for Art Riedel, owner of Willamette Tug and Barge Co., long before he ran the *Portland*. Once he was her captain, he kept the *Portland* fit and ready for any job on the water for over 8 years. Even though it took 2 hours to fire her up, the *Portland* was in great shape and could still outmaneuver any other tug with Captain Russell at the wheel.

The Portland on a ship assist transfer.   (Capt. Dale Russell Collection)

Prior to her last day of service, a newspaper advertisement carried a coupon inviting their readers to enter a drawing. Those lucky people, who were chosen from the thousands of tickets, got to ride on the steamer on her last cruise day and an extravagant retirement party. So, rather than towing giant ships, the *Portland* made five one-hour cruises up and down the Willamette River with 250 passengers on each run.

Captain Russel was the last captain to run the *Portland* when she was a working boat. When the *Portland* sternwheeler was retired, Captain Dale Russell, a river man for 40 years, said he will miss her and the people of Portland will lose the beautiful chuff of her whistle as she huffs and puffs on the water. He knew she was too expensive to run with a 7-member crew. She took more fuel than the new diesel tugs, which required only two men to run the vessel.

Captains Larry Baumfalk, Dale Russell, and Ray Ringering, on the decommission cruise of 1981. (Capt. Dale Russell Collection)

Captain Jack Taylor:

Captain Dennis Brown, Richard Montgomery, William Bach, and Captain Jack Taylor on the Portland. (Oregon Maritime Museum Collection)

Born and raised in California as a farm boy, Jack's life was dramatically changed when World War II broke out. At first, he wasn't old enough to be enlisted, but in 1942, Jack was accepted into the V-12 Navy Reserve program. (The V-12 was a program where the enlisted were sent to college and studied engineering and a set of military courses.) Jack earned his commission as an Ensign in July of 1945 from the Navy Midshipman School at Notre Dame University.

In September of 1945, Jack was sent to the Algiers Naval Base in New Orleans, where he was assigned to a small 150-foot long harbor freighter, the *YF 879*. Jack became the Executive Officer under one captain on board; soon they left for the San Francisco Bay area. When the captain was discharged, another one took his place. After the second discharge, Jack was left as the captain. Captain Taylor oversaw a crew of 16 men. His ship collected small arms ammunition and anti-aircraft shells from returning small boats and landing ships. (During World War II, the U.S. Navy ammunition ships were converted from merchant ships or specifically modified merchant ship hulls, often C-2 cargo ships. They were armed and were manned by Navy crews. Several of them were destroyed in spectacular explosions throughout the war. Notable among them was the *USS Mount Hood*, which was destroyed in the Admiralty Islands on November 10, 1944.)

Everything was then taken to the Mare Island Naval Base in Vallejo, California. Captain Taylor was discharged in July of 1946; his years in the military were a great learning experience as he had never been on any boat before the Navy.

After Jack was home for a few months, he looked up a friend he had met in Midshipman School. Bob Thomayer's wife's family was in the tug and barge business on the Willamette and Columbia Rivers. His friend invited him up to Oregon and put him to work for the Russell Towboat and Moorage Co. (which later became the Tidewater Barge Line in 1947). The first thing Jack had to do was get his certification to be an officer on their tugs. Jack got his Pilot's license in 1950 and his Master Mariners' License in 1951.

Captain Taylor ran tugs on all parts of the northwest rivers. He went as far as the McNary Dam hauling petroleum, and Albany, Oregon, where he worked for the Albany Barge Lines, a subsidiary of Russell Towboat and Moorage Co. In 1964, he went to work for the Willamette Tug and Barge Company in Portland. While with them, he ran ship-assist tugs and hauled gravel.

In 1968, Art Riedel, Jr., the president of Willamette Tug, attained the contract to manage the ship-assist sternwheeler tug *Portland* from the Port of Portland. Since running a steamer required a licensed Master and a licensed Chief Engineer, both Captains Taylor and Sam Gear were the only qualified men at Willamette Tug to work the *Portland*. Sam became the captain and Jack the mate and student pilot. Jack soon graduated up to captain again and ran the sternwheeler.

The *Portland* was a stepping-stone for Captain Taylor to be invited to join the Columbia River Pilots. (River pilots are licensed by the state of Oregon to provide pilotage services for the maritime industry.) He had been watched by current pilots and noted for his ability in maneuvering the *Portland* through the waters. Captain Taylor became a member in 1972.

Over these years, Captain Taylor's most prized work was running the *Portland*. She was a challenge and a lot of work keeping her smooth on the water moving ships on and off drydocks and shifting vessels from berth to berth. Capt. Taylor served as a Columbia River Pilot for 17 years and retired in 1989. He kept his license active for another 20 years.

Here is the Portland on the Willamette River helping to guide the Titan ship through the Broadway Bridge on the Willamette River in Portland. Below, she is helping the Forester go through the Burnside Bridge on the Willamette.

(Oregon Maritime Museum Collection)

With many years of service behind her, the *Portland* was becoming worn and outdated. She soon became a symbol of the old steamboat era. New barges were bringing in loads of containers to be stacked directly onto trucks, and they would be loaded with freight to take back to their homeport. They no longer needed the guidance of a small sternwheeler.

The Port of Portland's new floating drydock was put into service in 1979. This took over the ship repair business of the Alaska oil tanker fleet: large super tankers, some more than 1000 feet long, much too large for the *Portland* to handle alone. Even larger container ships worked out of the Port's out harbors; these ships did not need any tug pilotage.

(Zidell Marine Corporation Collection)

The *Portland* was expensive to use, more so than the more powerful tugs using the new propulsion systems. By 1981, any hopes of keeping her as a working assist tug were soon becoming no longer practical. She was officially retired on October 31, 1981.

The Port of Portland discussed ways to give the old sternwheeler a useful retirement. Neither the Port nor the Commission wanted to send her to the shipbreakers. Some of the ideas were to sell or lease her to a private operator as a passenger tour boat or tie her up as a floating maritime museum on the west side of the Steel Bridge. Both plans fell through.

Two marine operators thought about fitting her up for passenger service, but the cost of replacing the wooden house structure with steel to meet the U. S. Coast Guard safety requirements would be far beyond any profit after cost. The last restoration plan was believed to be from the Port of Portland who prepared the sternwheeler for a new purpose. This arrangement involved removing her wheelhouse and the 11 by 13 feet Texas in one piece and setting it on the beach. The wooden deckhouse that was the crew's quarters was already ruined. The house had too much dry rot and was in poor condition, as was the wooden superstructure that had rotted all the way down to the steel housing of her machinery space. This left the *Portland* with only her steel engine and boiler room house still on the hull. The Port had planned to make her a cruise boat, but in the end, it was too costly and the *Portland* deteriorated at Terminal 1 for ten years. Her exposed construction quickly weakened. Her once powerful stern wheel dried out and cracked where exposed to the air, and underwater it grew long tendrils of marine plants. It was a sad sight.

In 1985, four years after the *Portland* had been decommissioned, the Port of Portland still had plans to make her into an excursion steamer. The *Portland* was deteriorating into pieces, so they put together a voluntary group that generated two sets of archival photographs and abridged scale copies of the original working drawings and the conversion plans that had never been used. These documents were shown to the State Historic Preservation Office for its records, the Oregon Historical Society in Portland and the University of Oregon Library in Eugene. None of these agencies had the funds or supplies to keep the *Portland* active on the water.

In the spring of 1989, several Columbia River Pilots and previous captains of the boat made plans to save the sternwheeler. Captains Bill Petersen, Jack Taylor, and Dave Kasch (a river pilot for 41 years) helped launch an effort to resurrect it. By this time, the Oregon Maritime Center & Museum (OMC&M) had been created and was open to the public. Captain Peterson was president of the OMC&M; he and the volunteers wanted to restore the *Portland* for use as a maritime museum. Rick Boggs, an electrician, and several members of the museum formed a committee to meet with the Port of Portland.

The Port still had plans to save the boat from the scrapyard, so in 1991 they sold the *Portland* to the museum for $1. The Port also gave the Oregon Maritime Center & Museum the funds to begin a full restoration of this precious steam sternwheeler. It would take years to restore her back to working condition.

The museum membership undertook the enormous task of a complete restoration of this shattered steamer with a group of volunteers: active and retired mariners, river pilots, sea scouts and other interested people. As they examined the pilothouse and Texas deck, placed on blocks outside Terminal 1, they soon saw too much dry rot from it sitting neglected outdoors.

Both Captains Peterson and Taylor reported the roof, foundation timbers, corner posts, window sills, and side walls were horribly rotted and would all have to be replaced with new wood. Rust, oxidization, and asbestos had to be removed from the boiler, engines and auxiliaries. The sternwheeler needed to be painted both interior and her exterior, new insulation and lubrication had to be applied in numerous places. The wheelhouse and the Texas would need to be reinstalled. Water lines, electrical cables, steering and communications had to be refurbished. The volunteers tackled these jobs with passion, meeting every Wednesday and Saturday with their hammers and saws.

The hull, with steel sides and machinery was postponed for another time. The work began on renovating the two houses onshore, and then they would move on to the hull of the sternwheeler and the rusting upper deck. The cabin deck had been ruined during the first renovation attempts and only a few panels had been saved. A new wood-framed cabin was created with steel reinforcement and later fitted out to be used as a meeting or conference room.

Once enclosed, the sternwheeler would require installation of heating and air conditioning systems, automatic sprinklers for fire protection, overhauling of engines, pumps, electrical generators, dry docking and sandblasting of the hull, water and sewer hook ups and moorings, all adding an immense cost to make the *Portland* like what she once was on the water. Captain Peterson estimated a total cost of $350,000. The museum's board of directors wanted public donations to meet most of this cost so they went to work on campaigning for the sake of the *Portland*.

The Port offered the use of the old Terminal 1 as a base for their work and donated $200,000 to the effort. As the work moved forward, the community offered more support in the form of materials and expert assistance. Still, the museum group was short of resources until the Fred Meyer Memorial Trust donated $300,000.

This was just the beginning of the prep work before the restoration.
(Oregon Maritime Museum Collection)

While the dredge crew fired the boiler on occasion and exercised the machinery, there was lots of refurbishing to do. A volunteer group was organized and the work went on nearly 24 hours each day. It started with establishing a drydock and bottom painting of the hull. Other volunteers focused on the engines, replacing gears in the steering mechanism, and laying new lines. Others were very busy collecting more money for the restoration. All of the people involved in this project thought it would take only a few months to restore this sternwheeler. Instead, it lasted years. This enthusiasm so impressed the Port that they helped the Museum by applying for grants from the Meyer Memorial Trust and the Murdock Trust for funds to build a new deckhouse, assemble the Pilothouse and stack in order to make her a complete boat again. Nevertheless, it still seemed to be an impossible project.

By using sets of archival photographs and scale copies of original working drawings, the museum and its volunteers did their best to keep the *Portland* as close to what she was in 1947. Aside from the new regulations, safety, useful modern equipment, and comforts they kept her look as original as they could. They restored and replaced the same number of windows all like the original. They did have to modify to shore codes, not marine codes, as the *Portland* was now a shore side attraction.

Captain Taylor was in charge of all the initial work on the boat. He oversaw the change from the original steam coiled radiators that burned black oil to a new diesel burning system.

Ron Youngman, a retired U.S. Coast Guard commander, was in charge of all operations and maintenance of the boat. Over the next four years, hundreds of volunteers put in some 30,000 hours labor in restoration work.

The hull became a massive refinishing project.
(Oregon Maritime Museum Collection)

There was still much to do however – from replacing the timbers on the 25-foot diameter, 35-ton, wooden sternwheel to repairing the firebox.

(Oregon Maritime Museum Collection)

In May 1992, the Portland was towed upriver to join the annual Rose Festival fleet of US and Canadian warships. Nevertheless, there was still so much to do to restore the *Portland*, everything from replacing the timbers on the 25-foot diameter, 35-ton, wooden sternwheel to repairing the firebox. Parts had to be chiseled, scraped and painted, or replicated and replaced if they were too damaged. The boiler work culminated in re-certification and the first steam up. In 1993, the volunteers made the first self-powered trip in 12 years.

Just as the *Portland* was in operating condition (yet still not fully restored), the news had reached the movie company, Warner Bros. This historical steam sternwheeler was exactly what they needed and negotiations quickly began between the studio and the Oregon Maritime Museum. The *Portland* had only taken her maiden voyage on June 6 that year and a couple of short test runs and staff cruises, but they didn't turn down the opportunity to be in the upcoming movie, *Maverick*.

Warner Bros. planned to transform the *Portland* into a Mississippi style gambling sternwheeler: the *Lauren Belle*, queen of the western rivers. In just a few short weeks, she was dolled up with gingerbread designs, plus two smoke emitting dummy stacks. Soon, actors Mel Gibson, Jodi Foster, and James Garner, (who played the original *Maverick* character in the television series) were on board playing sly and sneaky gamblers.

Captain Dave Cash, Captain Jack Taylor on standby, and the rest of the crew performed all the operations of the *Portland* during her scenes and transportation. They were also paid for their work.

Since the movie props were fragile, they did not want the boat to run anymore before the actual shooting of the film. So on the selected day, she set out for Dodson, Oregon, (about 4½ miles east of Multnomah Falls and one mile west of Warrendale) which was the base of location for these movie scenes. When she left her dock, she lost one feed water pump and the second one quit when she landed. The first pump was damaged and was not repairable. A bolt had loosened on the second pump: an easy fix.

The *Portland* was outstanding and smooth for the rest of the trip. For the movie, she had to make many exhilarating and difficult moves, but both the crew and boat were perfect. The movie people did not know what different tasks they assigned, but they were carried out to their satisfaction. Once the filming of *Maverick* was finished, the *Portland* lost her theater garb and returned to her original look.

The Portland was made to look like the fictional Lauren Belle sternwheeler for the movie, Maverick.

(Oregon Maritime Museum Collection)

In 1996, the Willamette Valley Flood was part of a larger series of downpours all along the Pacific Northwest, taking place between late January and mid-February. It was Oregon's largest flood event in terms of losses and financial damage during the 1990s. On February 8, 1996, Captain Taylor controlled the *Portland* during current torrent along with Bill Peterson as the fireman. As the water rose up nearly 30 feet in the moorage, the men had to steam up that night just in case Captain Taylor had to take her away from the dock and out under the Morrison Bridge to get her down the river. As the floodwater came within inches of overtopping the seawall and flooding into Portland's downtown Tom McCall Waterfront Park, next to the *Portland*, Captain Taylor had to move her - and fast!

They were directed to line up and go through all the now open bridges. After getting into the open water, he tried to take her over to Swan Island, but the currents wouldn't let him. Captain Taylor had to slide her into the emergency berth where the water was still rising, but the dock remained above the water line. Soon, the barge went under the water. Volunteers had to pull the barge. The *Portland* was kept at Swan Island for a few weeks until it was safe for her to return to her moorage.

Later that year, the *Portland* steamed from her moorage at the seawall to become the leading attraction at the Antique and Classic Boat Show. That same year she assisted the restored Liberty ship *Jeremiah O'Brien* by guiding it from the mouth of the Willamette River to the harbor. Once there, she assisted the *O'Brien* in docking at the seawall.

When the museum was ready to make public its sternwheeler in 2001, the U. S. Coast Guard changed the ship's status to a boat for hire, which required another overhaul. This new status set the group back another seven years on their work.

The museum board chose a trip on June 27 in 2008 for their inaugural trip. They would go from Portland to the Cascade Locks. Once there, the *Portland* would compete against their regular opponent, the diesel-powered sternwheeler, the *Columbia Gorge*.

The U. S. Coast Guard issued a temporary permit to the museum for the *Portland* to take paying passengers for the day of the race. The museum sold tickets, at a $150 for the round trip cruise, primarily to museum board members, volunteers and their families. At the tiller was Paul Simonis, a ship captain who had owned and ran the sternwheeler *Rose* and held the proper license to run this sternwheeler. Up in the wheelhouse were Captain Taylor and Ron Youngman.

Since then, the *Portland* returned to quieter ways. Today, she is probably the last functioning commercially running steam-driven sternwheeler in the world.

She is the sole remaining steam-powered tugboat built and worked in America still active on the water. To the volunteer captains, pilots and crew, she is a needed harbor tool. To the historians and eager visitors, she is the symbol of a permanent reminder of the half a thousand steamboats that worked for more than a century on the rivers of Oregon.

You can visit the Oregon Maritime Museum (formerly called the Oregon Maritime Center and Museum) on the *Portland* and enjoy its location as well. The moorage is held by attachment to a floating petroleum barge that is fastened to two reinforcements or vertical I beams affixed to the seawall. Held fast, the *Portland* and connecting barge may rise and fall with the river. The 35 by 166-foot steel barge, built by the Brooklyn Navy yard in 1944, used during World War II, was eventually gained by a Columbia River barge line, and renamed the *Russell No. 24*. It was transferred to the Oregon Maritime Center and Museum in 1992, and while its recent history is associated with Columbia basin shipping, it is not related to the Port of Portland functions and is counted a compatible, noncontributing feature.

The *Portland* meets the National Register Criterion C because she is an exceptional representative of her specific category of sternwheeler and her engineering and naval architecture. She was entered into the National Register of Historic Places on August 14, 1997, in Multnomah County, Oregon. She was awarded this honor because of the importance of her being built and launched in 1947 and her powerful engines, length, her system of four main and three outboard rudders, and her paddle wheel. Her rudders allowed her to move with target maneuverability and her paddlewheel gave the *Portland* the ability to use leverage to aid disabled vessels many times her size and tonnage. The *Portland* was designed to be secured alongside her tow and move with it as a single component.

APPENDIX A: THE OREGON MARITIME MUSEUM

The Oregon Maritime Museum (OMM) developed over an interest and respect of our nautical Northwest history. The founders of the OMM came from two different organizations; formed in the mid-1970s, the Nautical Society of Oregon (NSO) and Northwest Seaport (originally, S.O.S., Save Our Ships) were trying to save *Lightship No. 83* (later renamed *Swiftsure*). These hardy founders came from different backgrounds, but they all were interested in forming a maritime center or museum. Captain Bill Peterson and Dr. Everett Jones from the NSO met with Captain Bill Speidel, Lloyd Knudson, and E. R. "Dell" Ricks from the lightship group; they formed an alliance together. The Oregon Maritime Center & Museum association was organized and adopted by these seamen in October of 1980.

With their vast experience, these men developed the museum project and saw it through to completion. Mr. Lloyd Knudson, the museum's first president, had served in the Navy as a seaman during WWII and later served as the Executive Secretary of the Maritime Metal Trades Union. Captain Speidel had been a long time river pilot on both the Columbia and Willamette Rivers. He was supportive of saving the lightship *Swiftsure*. Captain Bill Peterson was a graduate of the Naval Academy and had been a fighter pilot during both the Korean and Vietnam Wars. He was a maritime artifact collector specializing in naval instruments. (His collection was one of the most well known in the United States.) Dr. Everett Jones served as a Medical Corpsman aboard U.S. Army and Navy troop transports during WWII. Like Captain Peterson, Dr. Jones was a maritime relic collector, but his were more in the line of paintings, books, ship models and hardware.

The museum opened on October 29, 1986, in the historic Smith Building at 10 SW Ash Street, along the waterfront in Portland, Oregon. Their collections, along with many wonderful pieces from Mrs. Ruth Brandt and many fine ship models from Mr. Ed Neubauer and Mr. Dave Engen, decorated the museum.

After establishing a reputable maritime museum, their next project became the salvage and restoration of the sternwheeler steamer, the *Portland* in 1990 - 1993. Ron Youngman, both a charter member of the museum and a retired commander of the U.S. Coast Guard, helped develop the "Black Gang," a group of volunteer engineers that took on the renovation of the sternwheeler *Portland*.

After their successful restoration, the museum is now stationed in the *Portland* sternwheeler, parallel berthed at the seawall on the west bank of the Willamette River at the foot of SW Pine Street, near Governor Tom McCall Waterfront Park, opposite the museum's home base at 113 SW Front Avenue in Portland, Oregon.

APPENDIX B:
PORTLAND STEAMER STERNWHEELER TECHNICAL DATA

The Hull:

The hull is of all welded steel construction, butt welded. It is transversely framed from frames 0 - 19 and longitudinally framed from frames 19 to 93. The keel plate is 3/8 inch by 5 feet and extends full length of the vessel aft of frame seven. There is a forged steel forefoot 1½ by 6 inches in section. The transom is of 5/16 inch plate with 4 x 3 inches by 5/16 inch angle stiffeners. The transverse framing is of 4 x 3 inches by ¼-inch angles and the longitudinal frames are of 4 x 3 inches by 5/16 inch angles on 21-inch centers.

Longitudinal girders are of 5/16 inch flanged plate and are 7 feet and 14 feet off center, port and starboard. Bilge stringers are 5 x 3 inches by 5/16 inch angle and dock stringers 6 inches, 10.5 pounds.

W. T. and/or O. T. bulkheads are at frames 8, 19, 43, 53, 63, 73, and 85. Bulkheads are of 5/16 inch and a ¼-inch plate with 3 x 2 inches angle stiffeners in 24-inch centers.

Fuel oil tanks are between frames 8 - 19 and 43 - 53, feed water tanks between frames 54 - 63. Two independent potable water tanks are in the wings, port, and starboard.

Shell plating is of 5/16 inch steel with a 3/8 inch plate sheer strake, all butt welded.

Deck plating is ¼ inch, butt welded.

Two longitudinal trusses are above the main deck extending from frames 19 aft to the stern wheel support. These trusses are built up of 8 inch H-beams and 6 x 4 inch angles.

The engine girders are of ½-inch plate and extend from the shell bottom to above the main deck and from frame 73 to the fantail girder.

12-inch channels from the gunnel strake are fitted with 4 inch x 12 inch inside guard timbers faced with 4 inch x 1-foot oak. A split pipe fender is 4 feet below the shear line.

The Deckhouse:

The main deckhouse, extending from frame 19 to the transom is an open area housing the boilers, main propulsion engines, auxiliaries, and so forth. Storerooms and washrooms are included.

Walls are of 3/16 inches overhead of 5 pounds. Plate: two 5½ feet x 8½ feet, steel sliding doors are on the forward end, two 8½ feet x 8½ feet amidships, port, and starboard.

The *Portland* is a towboat. Her port and starboard winches and tackle blocks lash her so securely to a tow that she literally becomes that ship's own rudder and motive system.

Cabin Deckhouse:

The cabin deckhouse, extending from the frame 19½ feet to 73½ feet is constructed of tongue and groove wood. This cabin houses the docking, mess and lounge quarters for the crew. The lounge area is at the forward end equipped with tables, settees, etc. At the back of this space are staterooms for thirteen people in single and double spaces, each fitted with steel lockers and built in bunks. The galley is behind the canteen and is fully equipped with all the needed amenities, including oil burning stove, stainless steel sinks, and cabinets.

In separate houses behind the galley is the refrigerator, ice storage space and the dry galley storeroom. All interior rooms are covered with battleship gray linoleum.

Texas Deckhouse:

The Texas Deckhouse provides space for the Captain, Mate, Pilot, and a spare. The exterior deck is made of tongue and groove construction with a canvas; the interior deck covering is linoleum.

Pilothouse:

The pilothouse is above the Texas deckhouse and is approximately 11 feet by 13 feet. In it are the hand and power steering wheels, engine room telegraph, bell pulls, chart table, and navigating equipment. With the large windows on each side of the pilothouse, one has a full view from the steamer.

Machinery

Steam Plant:

On the *Portland* are two oil-fired, cross drum, sectional header, Babcock and Wilcox boilers, each has a steam capacity of 22,000 lbs. hr. at 250 psi using feed water supplied at 200 degree Fahrenheit. Each boiler is fixed with three Babcock & Wilcox Decagon C.D.D.F. straight mechanical atomizing oil burners. Each boiler is fitted with Diamond soot blowers and L.J. Wing turbo blowers for induced draft. A Reliance "Eye - Hye" remote reading water level indicator is provided for each boiler behind at the engineer's station.

A unit-type oil plant is on the boiler flat containing 2 Worthington Duplex pumps, Coen-Multiform heaters, and twin suction and discharge strainers. Full transfer is provided between oil tanks and each one is furnished with a "Levelometer" remote reading gauge.

Feed water is delivered by two horizontal end-packed pot valve plunger duplex pumps, drawing water from the feed tanks or direct from the river. Three Renauld heaters, each having a capacity of 22,000 lbs. hr. at 200 degree Fahrenheit, are given steam from bypassed exhaust lines of the main and auxiliary systems. Each boiler is fitted with a Copes feed water system and each pump has a Copes regulator.

Portland's two water drums supply the boilers with their working pressure. At the engineer's station is the steam cutoff lever (directly under the engine telegraph), a powered forward and reverse lever, and a manual forward and reverse lever in case the power system fails. The master gauge panel records steam pressure on both boilers and feed water pressure from the two water drums is two hundred fifty pounds per square inch.

Main Engines:

Northwest Marine Ironworks in Portland, Oregon, actually built the *Portland*, but the Central Brass Company, Western Steel Casting Company, and the Western Foundry Company all helped with replacing broken and missing parts. The engines were designed and built by the Northwest Marine Iron Works. The propelling engines are made from two sets of single cylinder, horizontal, non-condensing, reversing steam engines, operating at 235 psi. These engines are behind the main deck and drive two steel pitmans, which are connected, to the paddle wheel.

Each cylinder has a bore of 26 inches and a stroke of 108 inches. Valves are of the piston type and are adjustable as to points of admission, exhaust, compression, and cut off. The cut off valve is variable over the range from one quarter to full stroke. The valves are operated through eccentrics located inside the deckhouse and are driven by an arm activated by the pitmans. Link reversing gear is used.

Pitmans are made of welded steel box girder design, fitted with forged steel ends and u-straps. Bearings are made of cast bronze fitted with taper keys. Each pitman is 36 feet long with a crosshead bearing 7 inches in diameter and a crank bearing 9 inches in diameter.

All operating levers are at the engineer's station and include the main throttle, manual cut off, manual reverse, and power reverse. The power reverse is a single cylinder steam ram fitted with a compensating valve gear. All tumbler shafts are below the main deck.

120

The main throttle valve is of the semi-rotary type fitted with a pilot valve. The crankshaft is made of forged alloy steel, hollow bored with a 15½-inch diameter and 30½ feet long. Forged steel cranks with a 54-inch throw are at each end fitted with nickel steel shrunk in pins. Five wheel hubs are in the shaft, each 6 feet in diameter. The shaft works in two large pillow blocks on the engine girders. The paddle wheel is made of wood and is 25 feet in diameter, 26 feet wide. There are 20 buckets, 3 feet wide each.

Auxiliary Machinery:

The vessel is equipped with a Markey twin cylinder drum-type steering engine with pilothouse control activating the rudders through an 80-degree arc. There are four main rudders and three monkey rudders connected to the steering engine through a system of joining links, quadrant, and wire rope. The rudders are made of wood, balanced, and mounted of forged steel stocks with provision to ship or unship without docking. A 6-foot auxiliary steering wheel is in the pilothouse.

Four double drum friction operated reversing steam winches are provided for the handling lines. Two on the open forward main deck and two amidships in the main deckhouse. Winch cylinders are 7 inches by 1 foot with piston valves and fitted with a reversing valve. Each drum has a capacity of 1,475 feet of 7/8 inch wire rope with a designed line pull of 20,000 pounds. Each winch is supplied with a heavy-duty full swiveling fairlead mounted on a separate foundation. Winches and fairleads were designed and built by the Northwest Marine Iron Works.

A fire and general service pump is on the main deck and hydrants and hose connections are in the main, cabin, and Texas decks. This pump is fixed to draw water from the bilge or aft sea well, and to discharge overboard, to the fire lines, or to feed water tanks. A potable water pump is positioned in the main deck, drawing water from the tanks and discharging through both hot and cold water lines to the galley, staterooms, bath, and washrooms. A sanitary pump is furnished to draw water from the sea well and discharge to the sanitary system. All pumps are equipped with governors.

Steam syphons are in each hull compartment. Steam smothering lines are in the hull lamp and oil lockers. A fifty gallon hot water tank is installed, steam heated with thermostat control.

Electrical Systems:

A steam engine driven generator, direct current, self-excited, provides power two-wire compound wound 120-volt 15 kW capacity.

A dead-front switch is supplied, mounting all necessary busses, controls, etc., and is arranged to utilize ac current from shore when tied up. A standby generator (steam-driven turbine) is installed to provide current for the engine room telegraph and some lights in the event of the main plant being shut down. Four panel boards are located throughout for current distribution.

A 1000-watt pilothouse controlled searchlight is mounted on the pilothouse roof and four floodlights are on the cabin deck, fore and aft. The fire alarm system is an electrical bell type. Sound powered telephones are in the pilothouse, the boiler room, and the engineer's station. There is a repeat-back electrically operated engine room telegraph, also a trip gong and jingle bell system.

Miscellaneous:

The *Portland* Sternwheeler is equipped with a lifeboat and a workboat hung on davits and mounted in cradles on the back of the cabin deck. There are necessary navigational and safety equipment, including clocks, 8-inch compass, fog bell and horn, anchor, fire hose, life buoys, and much more.

The *Portland* Sternwheeler has the following attributes:

Length, stern to transom	186 feet
Length, overall	219 feet
Breadth, molded	42 feet
Depth, molded, at sheer line	9 feet
Shear, forward	3 feet 10½ inches
Shear, at transom	2 feet 1 inch
Camber	0 feet 9 inches
Designed mean draft, light	5 feet 3 inches
Designed mean draft, full load	5 feet 6 inches
Gross tonnage	928 tons
Net tonnage	733 tons
Fuel oil capacity	133 tons
Feed water capacity	80 tons
Potable water capacity	2 tons

(This information is from the *Commemorative Document Celebrating the Anniversary of the Oregon Maritime Center & Museum and Steam Sternwheeler, PORTLAND,* August 23 - 24, 1997.)

APPENDIX C: SOME OF THE EARLY NORTHWEST STEAMBOATS

ALERT: This sternwheeler was built in Oswego, Oregon, in 1865. The *Alert* was 135 feet long, (except for the extension of her main deck over the stern, called the "fantail" on which the sternwheel was mounted). She measured out at 340.83 gross tons. Her two single-cylinder steam engines were horizontally mounted, each one had a cylinder bore of 16.5 inches and a piston stroke of 60 inches. She worked on the Willamette River from 1865 to 1875. The Willamette Steam Navigation Co. originally owned her. The People's Transportation Company acquired it and rebuilt her in 1871. In 1875, the *Alert* was dismantled.

Herbert H. Holman in Portland, Oregon, built this sternwheeler for the America Transportation Co. in 1912. She was 105 feet in length with a beam of 18.5. She ran on the Portland – Astoria route. Here she is on the Willamette River near Portland.

(Oregon Maritime Museum Collection)

AMERICA: M. H. Higgins built the steamer *America* in Portland for Herbert H. Holman's American Transportation Company in 1912. She was 97 tons with a 150 horsepower engine. Five men ran the steamer while she transported cargo along the west coast. In 1942, her engines were removed. She was burned near the mouth of the Willamette River in 1946.

ANNIE FAXON: The sternwheeler *Annie Faxon* was built by the Oregon Steam Navigation Company in Celilo in 1877, and then rebuilt in Texas Ferry, Washington, in 1887. She was 165 feet in length and went from 709 tons down to 514. The Oregon Steam Navigation Company sold their stock to the Oregon Railway and Navigation Company in 1887 for a huge profit.

The *Annie Faxon* ran on the upper Columbia above Celilo Falls. She was one of the largest sternwheelers to work on these routes. She could navigate 141 miles up the Snake River to Lewiston, Idaho.

The *Annie Faxon* is most remembered for her boiler explosion on April 14, 1893, at 7:30 a.m. at Wade's Landing on the Snake River that destroyed her and killed eight people on board. The boat was coming in for a landing with Captain Harry Baughman in command. Suddenly, with no warning, the boiler exploded and the upper works of the steamer were demolished. The bride of purser J.E. Tappen was blown into the river and drowned. The boat's pilot, Thomas McIntosh, was beheaded by flying glass or metal, a deckhand was killed instantly on deck and the crewman William Kidd was blown to pieces. Captain Baughman, who had been standing next to pilot McIntosh, was blown out of the steamer and landed on the shore; amazingly, he was only dazed and injured. Seven crew members were killed, John McIntosh, Thomas McIntosh, William Kidd, Henry Bush, Pain Allen, George Farwell, and Scott McComb.

The hull of the *Annie Faxon* was recovered and used in the construction of the steamer *Lewiston.* In July of 1922, the *Lewiston* was destroyed by fire, as she lay moored at the Snake River Avenue landing in Lewiston, Idaho. The source of the explosion was later said to be the malfunction of a safety valve (called a "fusible plug"), designed to blow when the water level in the boiler fell too low. Not long before this trip, the steamer had been inspected, and while she was 16 years old, just six years before, she had been rebuilt in 1887.

This was a typical passenger steamboat of the Puget Sound Mosquito Fleet. The Athlon was built in Portland, Oregon, by the J.H. Johnston yard. She was launched in 1900. (Shaver Transportation Collection)

ATHLON: This vessel was just your average passenger steamboat made in the Northwest, USA. At the price of $4,950, she had been built in Portland in 1900 at the J. H. Johnston yard for the conglomerate of Jacob Kamm, owner of the Vancouver Transportation Company, the Shaver Transportation Company, and the Kellogg Transportation Company. This business group planned to use the *Athlon* in direct competition with Captain Neusome and his steamer, the *Iralda*. With two passenger boats now working on the Columbia River, it gave a fair price to eager customers. After some time, the *Athlon* was sold to H. B. Kennedy who took her up to Puget Sound, Washington. The *Athlon* then became a part of the Puget Sound Mosquito Fleet. In a dense fog on August 1, 1921, while she was going to Port Ludlow, the *Athlon* smashed into the Ludlow Rocks at the harbor's entrance. All nine people on board were rescued, but the steamer was a total loss. Poulsbo Transportation Co., her owners, reused her machinery on other boats.

BAILEY GATZERT: Her construction began in 1890, but wasn't complete until 1892. At 500 tons and 177 feet in length, the *Gatzert* was launched on the Columbia River and was the first wood-fueled steamer built to carry passengers. She was an elegant looking sternwheeler and was the fastest steamer on the Columbia during her time. In 1907, she was rebuilt and did not look like the original sternwheeler. Her lines were entirely different and the rooms on the hurricane deck had been removed. Her hull was longer than the original by 17 feet and her tonnage increased to 878. The new *Gatzert* was built like a steam schooner. The new sternwheeler was from the Regulator Line for work in the Portland Shipyards. During the Lewis & Clark Exposition, the *Gatzert* made twice daily runs from Portland to the Cascade Locks. She continued to run routes from Portland and Astoria, the lower Cascades, and The Dalles until 1907. She was then rebuilt and in 1917 sent up north to Seattle to work as a car and passenger ferry until she was abandoned in 1926.

BELLE: The sidewheeler, *Belle of Oregon City*, was another iron hulled boat built completely in Oregon in 1853, where she was launched from Oregon City. Captain William H. Troup had the steamer built for two other men, Captain W. B. Wells and Captain Richard Williams.

The *Belle* was a very distinguished steamer because everything, from the iron sheets that shaped her hull, her engines and all of her machinery, was of iron that had been worked in Oregon at a foundry owned by Thomas V. Smith. Smith had come out to Oregon from Baltimore to set up his own business and created the first iron steamboat built entirely on the Pacific Coast. The *Belle* was 90 feet long, 54 tons with a 16-foot beam and a deck with wide guards that gave her an overall length of 96 feet. She had plenty of room for her side wheels.

Because of her iron hull, she was much more resilient to the rivers than most early Northwest steamboats. When the Oregon Steam Navigation Company was created, the *Belle* was absorbed into its monopoly on the Columbia River; she was rarely used in their service. The *Belle* lasted until 1869 when she was scrapped. Her hull was dismantled and shipped to China and her engines went to power a sawmill in Oak Point, Washington.

CAPITAL CITY: originally named the *Dalton*, this sternwheeler was built at Port Blakely, Bainbridge Island, Washington, in 1898. Several companies, including, S. Wiley Steamship & Navigation Co., McDonald Steamship Co., Olympia - Tacoma Navigation Co, and the Dallas, Portland & Astoria Navigation Co. owned her. She went out of service in 1919 and was abandoned.

CARRIE LADD: John T. Thomas built the *Carrie Ladd* for Captain J. C. Ainsworth and Jacob Kamm in Oregon City in 1858; she was launched in October. The *Carrie Ladd* worked on both the Columbia and Willamette Rivers. She was one of the first steamboats specifically built with the Columbia River in mind. Unlike most other early steamboats, the *Carrie Ladd* was built from scratch, rather than from discarded hulls, works, or the machinery of earlier steamers. She was not particularly large: her dimensions were 126 feet in length, with a 24½-foot beam, and 4½-foot in depth of hold. The *Carrie Ladd* had powerful 16 by 66 inches engines (built in Wilmington, Delaware) and was probably the best of the steamboats built in Oregon in the 1850s.

The *Carrie Ladd* was originally planned for the Oregon City trade, but shortly after her completion the Union Transportation Company, (the forerunner of the Oregon Steam Navigation Company) was established, and the *Carrie Ladd* got the largest share given to any one steamer in that pool. Having superior power she found no trouble in going to the very foot of the rapids at the Cascades.

On June 3, 1862, the *Carrie Ladd* struck a rock near Cape Horn, 18 miles below the Cascades on the Columbia River and sank. Although she was raised and returned to work, she was never as durable. In 1864, she was transformed into a barge while her engines were reused in the sternwheeler *Nez Perce Chief.*

CASCADES: The Washington Territory Transportation Company built the sternwheel steamer *Cascades* in 1864, in Utsalady, Washington, on the Columbia River. When this was finished, they used her as a towing barge and dredges for the government. She was laid up and then later sold to Puget Sound for towing. She was then purchased by the North Pacific Lumber Company and brought down to Portland for use towing logs, but was not very profitable. The Shaver Transportation Company gained the *Cascades* tug in 1909 and kept her as a log and barge towing steamer and for occasional ship handling. They rebuilt her in 1912. She was used during World Wars I and II. The *Cascades* had an accident in 1943 when assisting a ship on Swan Island; she was burned beyond repair.

CHESTER: In 1897, the steamer *Chester* was 101 feet length, with a 20-foot 9-inch beam, and a 3-foot 8-inch depth of hold. Joseph Supple built her in his yard in Portland, Oregon, for Captains Oren, Ed, and Joseph Kellogg. She was a new design built specifically for the shallow waters. The *Chester* could navigate in a 1-foot channel. She was able to glide up onto the sand bars and spin her wheels to suck out the sand so she could crawl across. The *Chester*'s design was commonly used to build future shallow draft steamers, especially during the Klondike Gold Rush in Alaska (1896 – 1899).

She was made to work in the Cowlitz River above Kelso, Washington, where she connected with large vessels that were unable to work in low water. At many stops on the upper Cowlitz, her patrons drove their buggies and wagons alongside her to pick up and handover both freight and passengers. She continued to work on the Cowlitz River until 1910 when the river fell so low the channel was less than a foot deep. As the railroad and highway developments finally ended steamboat service on the Cowlitz in 1918, the *Chester* was left behind near Kelso Washington, in 1919.

The Claire made her last run with a farewell party. (Larry Barber Collection)

CLAIRE: Portland Shipbuilding Company in South Portland built the sternwheeler *Claire* in 1918 for the Western Transportation Company. The *Claire* was 157 feet long with a narrow 34-foot beam to allow her to go through the locks at West Linn; she had a 5½-foot depth of hold and was rated at 563 gross tons. She was built originally to tow log rafts and barges between the Crown Willamette Paper Company plant in West Linn, Oregon, the downtown Portland docks and the Crown Zellerbach plant in Camas, Washington, but in later years was relegated to barge pushing.

The *Claire* was so favored by the Veteran Steamboatmen's Association of the West that they borrowed her every last Sunday in June for their annual reunion at Champoeg Park. Between 150 and 200 passengers and many retired steamboat veterans working as crew would load up for a sixty-seven mile round trip from downtown Portland to the park. She made her last run upstream and through the locks in Oregon City to Champoeg on June 29, 1952.

L. Rex Gault, then president of Western Transportation Company, had her engines and boilers removed and retired the *Claire* to the company moorage as a floating shop. Her hull and exteriors were kept intact. Her famous three-bell whistle was transferred to the *Henderson*. Over the years, other pieces and equipment were removed.

On October 9, 1961, owners of the *Claire* set fire to the forty-three year old hull because they felt it was too far gone for further use and had become a fire hazard to the Western Moorage. So on a Columbia River sand bar near the lower end of Hayden Island, the *Claire* was removed forever from the waters. She was the last sternwheeler on the Upper Willamette River; the remaining three sternwheelers left on the river were too large to get through the locks.

COLONEL WRIGHT: R. R. Thompson and E. F. Coe in the Deschutes built the *Colonel Wright* in 1858. She was the first steamer sternwheeler on the Upper Columbia, covering the area from Celilo Falls to the Snake River. The *Colonel Wright* was 110 feet long, with a 21-foot beam, 12½ feet by 50-inch engines and a 5-foot depth of hold.

She was launched October 24, 1858, at the mouth of the Deschutes River. Initially these men ran smaller boats carrying freight for Fort Walla Walla from Celilo for a $100 a ton for freight. With this new steamer, they lowered the rate to $80 a ton. The *Colonel Wright*, which made three trips of full loads a week, made a fortune for her owners before others could interfere with the trade. They paid Captain Leonard White, who ran the steamer, a monthly salary of $500.

The *Colonel Wright* made her first trip in April of 1859 by connecting with the Oregon Steam Navigation steamers on the middle and lower Columbia River, landing passengers in Portland thirty hours after leaving Walla Walla; this achievement was amazing for this period of time. In May of 1859, the steamer made a surveying trip fifty miles up the Snake River and in 1861 ascended the Clearwater River to within two miles of the forks, completing the downstream run of over three hundred miles in less than 24 hours.

She made her last trip in the spring of 1865, under the command of Captain Thomas Stump, who tried to take her above the Snake River rapids to Farewell Bend. She was eight days in her journey of a distance of about one hundred miles; she was headed down stream and returned to Lewiston in less than five hours. Captain Stump reported his surveys as having been of no sensible worth, but he had taken a steamer farther into the heart of the regions lying to the east than any vessel had ever gone before. In August of 1865, she was dismantled at Celilo; her engines were later placed in one of Joseph Kellogg's other steamers.

COLUMBIA: R. R. Thompson and E. F. Coe built the *Columbia*. She was the first steamboat built in Oregon and was a namesake of the first craft to enter the Columbia River. Captain Daniel Frost, General John Adair, and the firm of Leonard & Green owned her. She was a small ferry type sidewheeler built at Upper Astoria. She was 90 feet long, with a 16-foot beam, a 4-foot depth of hold, and 75 tons burden. Her engines were of French make, noncondensing with an 8-inch bore and a 2-foot stroke. She could hold up to 20 passengers.

The *Columbia* made her trial trip at noon on July 3, 1850, with Captain Frost in command, Chief Engineer, Thomas V. Smith, Assistant Engineer, Henry McDermott, with Reuben Smith and Thomas Smith, Jr. on deck. She reached Portland at 3:00 p.m. the next day, and after anchoring there two or three hours, continued on to Oregon City, where she arrived about 8:00 in the evening, with a great jamboree being held in her honor.

Continuing in the commerce between Portland, Oregon City, Astoria, and Vancouver, the *Columbia* enjoyed a good business, fare and freight between river points being $25 per head or per ton. The running time between Portland and Astoria was 24 hours, the boat mooring up at night. As another lucrative source of income, she carried supplies from Vancouver to the Cascades, with occasional trips from Astoria with passengers from the Pacific Mail steamers, frequently carrying so many that there was hardly standing room on board. The owners once sent her 50 miles up the Snake River but the water was too shallow and swift; she only got as far as Lewiston during the 1861 freshet. The *Columbia* continued to be a transitory steamer until her engines were removed and placed in the steamer *Fashion.* The hull was swept away and lost during a June sea storm.

COWLITZ: The *Cowlitz* was a sternwheeler built by Milton Smith on the Tualatin River in 1917 for work on the Columbia River. She was 109 feet in length, with a 26-foot beam, carried 99 tons, and was 5½ feet in depth. In September of 1930, she was traveling downstream from The Dalles with a full cargo of wheat fighting severe 25 mph winds upstream that bucketed tons of water over her bow. The water flowed across her deck and ran into her engine room. Fires exploded and the *Cowlitz* sank. Luckily, her framework pulled free: the crew climbed aboard and rode it for more than an hour before being rescued.

DAISY AINSWORTH: The *Daisy Ainsworth* was a lavish sternwheeler steamer built in The Dalles in 1873 for the Cascades - The Dalles run. She was 177 feet in length and 673 tons. While most steamers seldom ran at night owing to the rock-strewn waters along the river, the *Daisy Ainsworth* was sent on a special run one night in 1876 to carry 210 head of choice beef cattle to the Cascades to be transferred to another craft for the Portland market. When nearing the Cascade landing in the pitch-black night, something went wrong and she slammed into the rocks, where most of the cattle drowned and she became a complete loss.

DALLES CITY: The *Dalles City*, 142 feet in length, was constructed in Portland in 1891 for the Portland - The Dalles run. She was rebuilt and lengthened by 10 feet in 1910 and renamed the *Diamond O* and worked up into the mid-1930s. She was one of four steamers (the others were the *Harvest Queen, Maria*, and the *Sarah Dixon*) to go through the Cascade Locks when it opened on November 5, 1896.

DIXIE THOMPSON: The sternwheeler *Dixie Thompson* was 155 feet in length and 443 tons, built by the Oregon Steam Navigation Company, and launched on January 2, 1871. Under the command of Captain Richard Hoyt, she ran the Astoria routes. Her first trip to Astoria was made in eight hours, which, according to the *Oregonian* newspaper, was the fastest time yet recorded in that direction. Although she had a variety of captains, the *Dixie Thompson* continued her work as a passenger steamer until 1881, and was later placed on the Cascade route in competition with the *Fleetwood*, then connecting with the *Gold Dust* above the Cascades. The Oregon Railway & Navigation steamer carried passengers for fifty cents each and, when that competition ended, the *Dixie* returned to the lower river as a freight boat. In 1885, she again worked on the Cascade route, continuing there under the charge of Captain John Wolf and A.B. Pillsbury until 1887, when Captain Henry Kindred ran her as a towboat. Charles Spinner, Edward Sullivan, and several other Oregon Railway & Navigation Company captains managed her in the towing business until 1893, when she was sent to the boneyard to be dismantled.

E. D. BAKER: The People's Transportation Company built this steamer in 1862. The *E. D. Baker* was 116 feet long, with a 25-foot beam, and a 6-foot depth of hold, with engines 16 by 72 inches. She was one of the fastest sternwheelers of her time, working on the Cascade route. With Captain E. W. Baughman in command, she was launched in Vancouver. The *E. D. Baker* made a few irregular trips on the Willamette River before she crashed and sank near Oswego the year after she was built. She was soon raised, but her hull was not repairable; her engines were removed and used in the sternwheeler *Reliance*, then later in the *Alice.*

ECHO: The *Echo* was a 122-foot sternwheeler built for the Willamette River Steam Navigation Company (WRSN) at Canemah, Oregon. She was launched May 22, 1865, and worked on the Willamette River until 1873.

The *Echo* was one of the first steamers to carry cargo out of Eugene to Portland. By April of 1869, the *Echo* was running on the Willamette between Eugene and Springfield, Oregon, carrying as much as 273 tons of cargo, which was then the heaviest freight ever embarked from Eugene. For a short time, the *Echo* was working above the Willamette Falls in conjunction with the screw-propelled steamer *U. S. Grant*, working below the falls. In March of 1866, the People's Navigation Company sometimes called the People's line, acquired WRSN and all of its vessels. In 1871, the People's line sold its assets to Ben Holladay's Oregon Steamship Company. The *Echo* was dismantled in 1873.

ELK: Captain Chris Sweitzer, Francois X. Matthieu, George Pease, and John Marshall built the *Elk* in 1857 in Canemah, Oregon. This sternwheeler was tiny. She was used for the Yamhill River trade. In November of 1861, the *Elk* was routing on the Willamette River near Davidson's Landing, which was about one mile below the mouth of the Yamhill River; officers on board were Captain George Jerome, engineer William Smith and the pilot, Sebastian "Bas" Miller. Suddenly her boiler exploded and the entire upper works of the sternwheeler collapsed. Although there were some injuries, no one was killed.

ELIZA ANDERSON: The *Eliza Anderson* was built by the Columbia River Steam Navigation Company and launched on November 27, 1858, in Portland, Oregon. She was a sidewheeler driven by a low-pressure boiler generating steam for a single cylinder walking beam steam engine. She was built completely of wood, measuring 197 feet long with a 25-foot 5-inch beam and rated at 276 tons capacity.

After her trial run on the lower Willamette and Columbia Rivers, she was sold to an association of John T. Bradford, some Canadian stockholders and three brothers: Tom, John T., and George S. Wright, who were early steamboat workers in the Pacific Northwest.

Following a steam pipe blast and crashing into a dock in Dutch Harbor, Alaska in 1897, the passengers and crew vacated her. During a terrible storm early in March, she broke from her anchorage and proceeded ashore before any help could be given her. She was left lying on her side with the tide flowing through several jagged holes in her base. The news of the *Eliza Anderson*'s wreck was brought to Seattle by the steamer *Bertha*. Her wreck in Alaska was a fitting end to her 40 year career, since she had so many times been rescued from the boneyard and put back into commission.

ELWOOD: This 154-foot in length, 510-ton sternwheeler steamer was built in 1891 for the Oregon Railway and Navigation Company for the Portland - Oregon City shuttle run. The *Elwood* was sold in 1894 to the Lewis River Transportation

Company and put to work on the Lewis River run. In 1903, she was running for new owners between Seattle and Tacoma.

ENTERPRISE(S): The first *Enterprise* was the first sternwheeler operating on the Upper Willamette River, built in the fall of 1855 by Archibald Jamison, Captain A. S. Murray, Armory Holbrook, and John Torrance. She was 115 feet in length, 15 feet in width, and worked on the Willamette River between Oregon City, Canemah, and Corvallis. In 1858, Jamieson sold her to Captain Thomas A. Wright. The next *Enterprise* was made in Canemah, Oregon, in 1863, with a length of 120 feet, a 24-foot beam, with a 4-foot depth of hold and 270 gross tons. Her engines were 14 by 48 inches. When the river conditions allowed her to, she ran between Canemah, Corvallis, and Harrisburg. Captain Pease and others owned this *Enterprise*; they dismantled her in Canemah, 1875. Another sternwheeler also called the *Enterprise* was built in Gardiner, Oregon, in 1870. She was left alone after a wreck in 1873. The next *Enterprise* was constructed in Astoria, Oregon, in 1883. She was a small sternwheeler, only 81 feet in length, and could carry only 94 tons. She was dismantled in 1902. Yet, another *Enterprise* was manufactured in Portland, Oregon, in 1890. This sternwheeler was 106 feet in length and 137 gross tons. She was rebuilt in 1902, increasing her length by 9 feet and boosting her tonnage to 333. This *Enterprise* was abandoned in 1916. Finally, the last historical northwest sternwheeler called the *Enterprise* was built in Wenatchee, Washington, in 1903. She was 86 feet in length and 129 gross tons. She was wrecked in 1915.

EVA: The passenger-carrying sternwheeler *Eva* worked on the Umpqua River on the Oregon coast in the early 1900s. She was built in 1884 in Portland. She was 90.4 feet long, with a beam of 19.4 feet, and a 4.6-foot depth of hold. The *Eva* measured out at 130.57 gross tons. Her draft was 2.5 feet. The *Eva* was powered with two steam engines, horizontally mounted, driving a sternwheel. She is most famous for her use by Oscar Hinsdale, one of her owners, to smuggle dynamite for stump-blasting purposes, labeled in boxes of "bacon."

FASHION: The sidewheeler *Fashion* was built in 1853. She was once the steamer *James P. Flint* with engines from the *Columbia*. She was a small boat, only 80 feet in length. Commanded by Captain J.O. Van Bergen, she covered several routes along the lower Columbia River going to the Cowlitz River on Monday and Tuesday, Oregon City Wednesday and Thursday, and the rest of the week to Vancouver and the Cascades. After running the Cascade route through 1856, she crashed into a reef (which later bore her name) and sank. She was raised and pumped out, patched, and continued to work until 1861 when she was robbed of her engine and left to rot.

F. B. JONES: The 143 feet in length, 303-ton freight and towing sternwheeler steamer was named after its owner, Mr. F. B. Jones. She was built in 1901 by T. Ellingson and was one of the three working boats for the Willamette & Columbia River Transportation Company (later taken over by the Shaver Transportation Company). She worked mostly on the Columbia River between Coal Creek slough (downriver from Longview, Washington) and the Cowlitz River towing log rafts and barge work for the Inman-Poulsen Lumber mills, located in Portland between the Hawthorne and Ross Island bridges. While working on a night run on the lower Columbia River, the boat was struck and sunk by the tank steamer *Asuncion*. She was later raised and repaired. The *F. B. Jones* was vacated in Portland in 1937.

The G. K. Wentworth berthed along the Columbia River.

(Shaver Transportation Collection)

G. K. WENTWORTH: This steamer sternwheeler was built in Portland, Oregon, by the Portland Shipbuilding Company Yards for the Hosford Transportation Company in 1905, and was launched in January of 1906. She was of the latest technology and was able to pull with any tow boats of equal power as well as pass them with her speed. She was the first sternwheeler to have steel cylinder timbers in the Northwest. Her length was 145½ feet with a 28 ½-foot beam, and had a 7-foot depth of hold, draft of 4 ½ feet, gross tonnage was 325 net, and net capacity 285 tons. Her engines had 72 stroke inches, bore 16 inches, and allowed 193 pounds steam pressure.

The *G. K. Wentworth* went to work towing logs and barges on both the Columbia and Willamette Rivers. She was abandoned in 1925, but was later dismantled in Portland in 1934 and her engines were used in the steamboat *Skagit Chief*, located up north in Puget Sound, Washington.

The G. W. Shaver is on the far left of the steamers that Shaver Transportation had moored along Portland's waterfront. Next to her are Sarah Dixon, No Wonder, and a small tug. (Shaver Transportation Collection)

G. W. SHAVER: This was the first sternwheeler tug built specifically for the Shaver Transportation Company. She was named after one of the founders, George W. Shaver. This sternwheeler was 140-foot in length and 313 gross tons. She was built in Portland in 1889. In 1902, she was renamed the *Glenola*, which later became the *Beaver* in 1905. This sternwheeler sank in 1935.

GAMECOCK: The sternwheeler *Gamecock* was 178 feet 2 inches in length, had a 38-foot beam, 772 gross tons and engines 18½ by 84 inches, high-pressure. The Shaver Transportation Company built her in 1898 in Portland for the Yukon Transportation and Commercial Company in Alaska. She was to be towed up north to Alaska to work on the Yukon River. After a short time in Alaska, the

Gamecock was returned to the Columbia River. One time she had been loaded with wood in the Columbia River and had passed over the bar, but could have sunk if the wood hadn't kept her afloat. After that, she was sold to the Willamette & Columbia River Towing Company and was used for freighting and towing.

In 1910, the *Gamecock* sank at Sheridan Point in the Cascade Rapids with a full load of wheat. She was reassembled exclusively for towing logs with new dimensions: 160 feet and 1 inch long, a 33-foot 5-inch beam, and the same engines from before. The *Gamecock* was regarded as one of the most powerful towboats on the river.

In the late 1920s she was refitted as a cross compound using one high-pressure cylinder, 18½ by 84 inches, and a low-pressure cylinder, 36 by 84 inches. She worked for a long and difficult time; she was dismantled in 1935. By 1938, what was left of her rotted away.

GAZELLE: The first *Gazelle* was built in Canemah in 1854. This 145-foot length sternwheeler steamer demanded a lot of room on the river. She made her first trip on March 18, 1854. On April 8 of 1858, while lying off the town of Canemah, her double engine boilers exploded, instantly killing over twenty people. Many more were wounded and four more victims died shortly afterwards. The *Gazelle*'s hull sank at the dock, but was later sold. Her new owners raised the hull, lined it over the Willamette Falls, and rebuilt it to become the *Sarah Hoyt*. The engines were later salvaged and installed in the *Senorita*.

A second *Gazelle* was constructed in Portland in 1876. She was a sternwheeler of 92 feet in length and 157 gross tons. She was transferred up north to Puget Sound in 1884.

The last historical *Gazelle* was built in 1905. She was a gas fueled small sidewheeler barely 92 feet in length and she could only carry up to 13 tons. She was deserted in 1929.

GEORGIE BURTON: The *Georgie Burton* was a sternwheeler 154 feet long, 31 feet wide, 382 gross tons, with engines of 16 by 72 inches and a 6½-foot depth of hold. She was assembled from the remains of the sternwheeler *Albany* in Vancouver, Washington, in 1906. The *Burton* was one of the last wooden steamboats on the Columbia River. She was rebuilt in 1923 in Portland, increasing her tonnage by 138, and used as a towboat for the Western Transportation Company. When departing, her whistle gave the traditional three-blast farewell to the people who waited on the riverbank to watch her pass by.

On March 20, 1947, she made a run from Portland to The Dalles; this was the last trip for the 41-year veteran steam-powered sternwheeler. (Although it may not have been the last steamboat trip on the Columbia, the news media reported that it was.) The *Burton* was secured up at the lower end of the Celilo Canal, with plans of turning her into a floating museum. Unfortunately, the Columbia River flood of 1947 broke her loose and floated the steamer over the wall and onto the rocks outside; she broke her back and became a total loss.

GOLDWATER: The merchants of Portland bought the 172-foot ocean steamship, the *Goldwater*. It served between Portland and San Francisco, with calls to Astoria and various coastal ports. The *Goldwater* was very profitable, running the Milwaukie and Oregon City ports for a sizable profit.

GOVERNOR GROVER: The sternwheeler *Governor Grover* was built in 1873 for the Willamette River Navigation Company. She was 120 feet in length and 404 gross tons. Because of the completion of the Willamette Falls Locks in 1872, boats of her size could be built in Oregon City, and then navigated above the falls. The *Grover* was named after Oregon's fourth governor, La Fayette Grover (1870 to 1877). She was launched on January 28, 1873, and made her first trip on March 16, that same year. Shortly after construction, she was purchased by the Willamette Falls Locks and Canal Company and worked on the Willamette River. The *Grover* pulled off some success in bringing down shipping rates, which was much liked by the farmers of the Willamette Valley.

The Willamette Falls Locks and Canal Company sold the *Grover* to the Oregon Steam Navigation Company, which used her on all of their routes running out of Portland. She was dismantled in 1880.

GRAHAMONA: The Yellow Stack Line in Joseph Supple's shipyard in Portland built the steamer *Grahamona* in 1912. Captain A. W. Graham, who owned the line, named her with one of the company's distinctive "ona" endings. She was one of the largest and finest sternwheelers to run on the Upper Willamette River. She had a length of 149 feet 5 inches, a 30-foot beam, carried 443 tons, and had 4 feet 5 inches depth of hold. Her engines were 14 by 72 inches. As a sternwheeler of the Oregon City Transportation Company, she carried thousands of passengers through the locks on the Willamette River. She was the last sternwheeler on the Upper Willamette River operating in a freight and passenger service.

By 1919, the *Grahamona* was transferred and refitted for use on both the Columbia and Snake Rivers, working with freight truck lines along the landings. In the late 1920s, after the Oregon City Transportation gave up working on the Willamette River, the Salem Navigation Company was formed. They bought the *Grahamona* and the following year renamed her *Northwestern*, using her as a floating crew barracks and workboat for the Pacific Telephone and Telegraph Company, stringing new cables in the Columbia Gorge. Later, she worked for a few more years between Portland and Salem on the same river. In 1939, the Salem Navigation Company sold her to Captain Wallace Langley, Alaska Rivers

Navigation Company of Juneau, for jobs on the Kuskokwim River of Alaska. The steamer was towed to Clallam Bay by the *Arthur Foss* with Captain Vince Miller and turned over to the active Captain L. H. (Leb) Curtis for the 2,611-mile tow to Goodnews Bay. Once there, she ran until 1949.

HARVEST QUEEN: The first *Harvest Queen* was a sternwheeler built in Celilo Falls in 1878 by the Oregon Steam Navigation Company. She was the largest steamer in the upper river; it weighed 846 tons, measured 200 feet with a 37-foot beam, a 7 ½-foot depth of hold, and her engines were 20 by 96 inches. The *Harvest Queen* was manned by Captain James W. Troup and worked above the Celilo Falls until 1881, during the completion of the railroad tracks by the Oregon Railroad & Navigation Company.

In February of 1881, under Captain Troup and engineers DeHuff and Pardun, she was taken down the Tumwater Rapids, one of the most thrilling trips ever made on the Columbia River. A week later, she was conveyed through the Little Dalles and later through the Big Dalles. In May of 1890, with 20 passengers on board, she was ferried down the Cascade Rapids with Captain Troup in charge. On this run, she covered the first 4 miles in just 4 minutes. She was one of four steamers to go through the Cascade Locks when it opened on November 5, 1896. The others were - *The Dalles City,* the *Maria,* (The *Maria* was built in Portland in 1887 and abandoned in 1923.) and the *Sarah Dixon*. The *Harvest Queen* was dismantled in 1899.

The second *Harvest Queen* was a sternwheeler built in 1900. She was 187 feet in length and 585 gross tons; she worked until she was retired in 1927.

HASSALO: The *Hassalo* (originally spelled *Hassaloe*) was the first sternwheeler built in the Cascades, Washington, and was 135 feet long, and a 19-foot beam, with a 5-foot depth of hold. She made her first trip in July of 1857, and was dismantled in 1865. The next *Hassalo* was built in The Dalles in 1880. She was 160 feet in length and 462 gross tons. She ran the middle river from 1880 to 1898; her first captain was Fred Wilson, followed by H.F. Coe, then Captain John McNulty for the last five years on the Columbia. The *Hassalo* became famous for running the Cascades of the Columbia on May 26, 1888, at a speed approaching 60 miles an hour. This steamer went to the Oregon Steam Navigation Company on the middle river and worked the Olympia - Tacoma - Seattle run in 1890. There, the *Hassalo* collided with the *Otter,* a much smaller sternwheeler, damaging the *Otter* beyond repair. In 1892, the *Hassalo* was returned to the Columbia River where she was converted to a towboat, serving there until 1898, when she was dismantled.

The last *Hassalo* was a sternwheeler built in 1899 in Portland. She was 181 feet in length and 561 gross tons. She was later transferred to Puget Sound, where under Captain O. A. Anderson she was stationed on the Bellingham route. This boat was dismantled in Portland in 1927.

The Hattie Bell on a run on the Willamette River.
(Oregon Maritime Museum Collection)

HATTIE BELLE: Built in Portland by Captain M. A. Hackett in 1892, the *Hattie Belle* was used as a towboat until 1894. The sternwheeler was sold for use on the Cascade route with the steamer *Ione*. The *Hattie Belle* was a small steamer; she was 110 feet in length, with a 24-foot beam, a 4.5-foot hold, and only 561 gross tons. She was dismantled in 1906.

HENDERSON: The long-lived Shaver Transportation Company sternwheeler, the *Henderson*, was built in the Portland Shipping Company and launched in 1909. She had many lives as she was sunk and rebuilt in 1912, rebuilt and reengineered in 1929, and then had her framing timbers and planking replaced in 1948. On December 11, 1950, while working along the side of Cottonwood Island, in the Columbia River near Rainer, Washington, she struck a submerged object that gave her a ragged tear in her hull. She sunk and was raised again. The *Henderson* was used in major towing work such as when for example, in the 1940s she was dispatched with four other towing vessels to pull the Standard Oil tanker *F.S. Follis* off from where the tanker had grounded near the mouth of the Willamette River.

The last days for the wooden hulled *Henderson* was in 1956 near Astoria, when she was damaged beyond her economic value in a collision with her tow.

IDAHO: The sidewheeler *Idaho* was used on the middle Columbia, Cascade Rapids to Celilo Falls from 1860 to 1989. John Holland built her on the Upper Cascades; she was 147 feet long, with a 26-foot beam, a 6-foot 9-inch depth of hold and 278 gross tons. She had been built in 1860 for Col. John S. Ruckel, and launched on December 9, by the Oregon Steam Navigation Company. Because the Cascade Rapids were not maneuverable, all traffic had to be routed around the rapids on portages. The *Idaho*'s job was to transport people and freight on the middle Columbia linked by the rapids; this was a very profitable run.

In 1861, Captain James Troup piloted her over the Cascades. In 1869, she was taken down to Portland and was completely rebuilt on a new hull. Her paddle wheels were replaced, while all new cabin space and a pilothouse were built. In 1881, she was sent around to Puget Sound to work in Tacoma, Washington. In May of 1984, she was sold to Captain D.B. Jackson who ran the Northwestern Steamship Company. He put her on the mail route from Seattle to Port Townsend. On August 10, 1894, she was sold to junk dealers, Cohn & Cohn. They removed her machinery, and then sold her to Dr. Alexander De Soto. Dr. De Soto placed the steamer up on pilings on the Seattle Waterfront to use as the town's first emergency hospital. When a new hospital was put in place in 1909, the *Idaho* was left to rot away.

IRALDA: The first *Iralda* was a wooden propeller steamer. She was 99 tons, 106 feet in length and fitted with triple expansion engines of 130 horsepower. The next *Iralda* was built in Portland for Captain W. S. Neusome in 1906. She was created from using parts of his original steamer.

The *Iralda* was a very fast steamer for both passenger and freight. She ran the Portland – Rainer - St. Helens route on the Columbia River. On her return, she would stop at the Willamette Slough, picking up milk and other dairy products for the Portland markets. In her later years, the Hosford Transportation Company owned the *Iralda*. Mr. L. H. Holman expanded her service to Astoria three days a week, charging from $1.50 to $2 each way. By 1921, her service was so popular, it created a rate war that dropped the Portland - Astoria fare down to $1.00. Because she was a light and sleek steamer, she could not keep up on working along the rough estuary of the Columbia River. She was deserted in 1932.

JAMES P. FLINT: The *James P. Flint* was built in 1851 and was the first wooden sidewheeler on the middle Columbia River. She was 80 feet in length with a beam of 12 feet. D. F. Bradford and Captain Van Bergen built her in the Cascades. After her completion, she was towed up over the Cascades to work in The Dalles, where there was an established military post. The following year she was moved to below the Cascades, and while under the command of Captain George Coffin in September, she was sunk opposite the Multnomah Falls. No lives were lost, but the craft was left alone until 1853, when she was taken to Vancouver and renamed the *Fashion*.

The Jean on the Columbia River. (Oregon Maritime Museum Collection)

JEAN: The sternwheeler *Jean* is the last semi intact sternwheeler to have worked on the Willamette River and the only one to have split paddlewheels. The paddlewheels were about 20 feet in diameter side-to-side, 16 feet wide at the axle, made of wood, and are estimated to weigh as much as 10 tons each. She also had a traditional hull formation made of steel, but she differed in her steering mechanisms and was less navigable. Commercial Iron Works in Portland built the *Jean* in 1938 for the Western Transportation Co., a subsidiary of Crown Zellerbach Corp. She was named after a daughter of a Crown Zellerbach executive. Originally, she was 140 feet long, with a 40-foot beam, a depth of hold of 7 feet 8 inches, 1200 horsepower engines and displaced 533 tons. She was designed by W. D. McLaren of Vancouver, British Columbia to tow logs and handle barges on both the Columbia and Willamette rivers. She worked until 1957. Stripped of her machinery and equipment, the *Jean* was left to rot in the Snake River near Lewiston, Idaho. The boat was last docked at the Port of Wilma, Washington, before making a journey of 365 miles to Portland, lashed to a grain barge and pushed by a tugboat where she will work as a response vessel.

JENNIE CLARK: Launched in February of 1855, the *Jennie Clark* was built on the same lot in Milwaukie, Oregon, that Captain J. C. Ainsworth and Jacob Kamm had built the sidewheeler *Lot Whitcomb*. The *Jennie Clark* was 115 feet in length, with an 18 ½-foot beam, 50 gross tons, and a 4-foot depth of hold. She was the first of hundreds of steam-powered sternwheelers to travel the Columbia River carrying passengers. The *Jennie Clark* was the earliest steamboat placed on the Portland - Oregon City route, with Ainsworth in command. He was so pleased with how she moved so smoothly over the Columbia River and how the sternwheel firmly pushed through the water with effective speed. Both he and Kamm turned her over to the Abernathy & Clark Company carrying the daily mail between Portland and Oregon City. The *Jennie Clark* was soon known as a fast and comfortable sternwheeler.

The *Jennie Clark* was bought and transferred over to the Oregon Steam Navigation Company. In 1862, she enjoyed the merit of being the first regular coastal vessel, making a weekly trip from Portland to Astoria's Clatsop Landing, partially running on the Lewis and Clark River (known as the Netul River until 1925). Because she had few passengers, the company removed her engines and transferred them to the *Forty-Nine*. The *Jennie Clark* was placed in the boneyard the following year. Her old hull remained until October of 1865, when it was burned for the iron. The *Jennie Clark* was a basic craft compared with the sternwheelers built after her. Ironically, by the 1870s, there were hundreds of customers traveling to and from Portland and Astoria.

J. N. TEAL: The Open River Transportation Co. in 1907 built this sternwheeler in Portland, Oregon. Her length was 160.7 feet, 35.4-foot beam, and a depth of hold at 5 feet. Both of her engines were 16 x 72inches. She was the first boat put to work carrying passengers and freight from Portland to Big Eddy, Oregon. The *J. N. Teal*'s last years of work were for the Willamette and Columbia Towing Co. She was abandoned in 1937 and was later dismantled.

JOSEPH KELLOGG: The sternwheeler steamer was originally built in 1881, and had been named after the ship builder and owner, Joseph Kellogg. She was only 128 feet in length and could carry 322 tons. Her machinery came from an old steamer, the *Dayton*, vintage of 1868. In 1900, Charles M. Nelson, the founder of the Portland Shipbuilding Company, rebuilt the *Joseph Kellogg*. It was increased to 462 gross tons and lengthened by 11 feet. In 1921, the *Kellogg* was renamed the *Madeline* and continued to work for another ten years.

LEWISTON: The O.R. & N. Company built the *Lewiston* in 1894 in Riparia, Washington, to replace the steamer *Annie Faxon*, which had been wrecked in a boiler explosion in 1893. Her dimensions were 165 feet in length, with a 34-foot 4-inch beam, a 5-foot depth of hold, engines 17 by 72 inches, and original tonnage 513. She was an excellent light draft sternwheeler in every respect. She adapted well for the Snake River. The *Lewiston* was rebuilt in 1905, increasing her power with 18 by 82 inch engines and an increase of 35 tonnage. In 1922, she caught on fire in Lewiston, Idaho, and was burned down.

In 1923, Joseph Supple built a new *Lewiston* in Portland. This sternwheeler was 160 feet in length, with a 35-foot beam, 18 by 84 inch engines, 581 tonnage and had a 6 ½-foot depth of hold. She continued to work on the Snake River until 1946, when the Western Transportation Company of Portland, who sent her down the Snake River on her farewell trip from Lewiston to Portland, purchased her. There, she was converted into a towing steamer, renamed the *Barry K*, and ran until she became a part of the United States Army for service on the Yukon River in Alaska.

LOGGER: In 1924, Smith Transportation Company in Rainer, Oregon, got hold of the laid up *Olympian*, stripped off the house and machinery, and installed them in a new 156-foot wooden hull. This new boat was 447 gross tons. She was built only to tow low rafts, and christened the *Logger*. The *Logger* was unique; she was the only sternwheeler ever built on the river to run hog fuel. (Hog fuel is chipped sawmill waste. It is dirty, splintery, and in all ways, nasty to the touch, but a cheap fuel.) After 1930, Shaver Transportation Company, which had obtained the *Logger* along with several other boats through a merger with the Smith Company, found running her was a constant problem and challenge. When she finally opened and sank at her moorings in 1938, no attempt was made to salvage her. She was stripped of anything useable and the hull now lies under many feet of fill that makes up the Waterway Terminals Company property on Portland's waterfront. Only her name board sits on display, preserved with many others in the marine museum in Champoeg, Oregon.

LOT WHITCOMB: The *Lot Whitcomb* was the first steamboat built on the Willamette River. She was launched on Christmas Day in 1850 from Milwaukie, Oregon, and named after the founder of the town. Her original owners were S. S. White, Berryman Jennings, and Lot Whitcomb. She was a luxurious sidewheeler, 160 feet long, with a 24-foot beam, 5-foot 8-inch depth of hold and 600 gross tons. Her paddle wheels were 18 feet wide. Her first crew was Captains J. C. Ainsworth and William L. Hanscome, Chief Engineer Jacob Kamm, Pilot W. H. H. Hall, and First Mate John H. Jackson. In 1854, she was transferred to California and later renamed the *Annie Abernethy*.

The Lurline on the Willamette River.   (Shaver Transportation Collection)

LURLINE: The sternwheeler, the *Lurline* worked both the Columbia and
Willamette Rivers from 1878 to 1930. Her builder, Jacob Kamm, launched her on
September 30, 1878; she was a typical steamboat of her time at 158 feet, a 30-foot
beam, a 6-foot depth of hold, and 481 gross tons. Captain James T. Gray
commanded her on the Vancouver route that she ran for the first ten years of her
career. During the summers, she made a trip each week on the seaside routes and
occasionally towed stranded vessels. The *Lurline*'s abilities often competed with
the Oregon Railway & Navigation Company (ORNC), costing them over a half a
million dollars in lost business. In 1889, the ORNC leased her under the command
of Captain Pillsbury. She worked the Cascades route until 1892 when Kamm put
her back on the Astoria trips under his son, Captain Charles T. Kamm.

In the early 1900s, the Harkins Transportation Company of Portland
bought her. Over those years, she was rebuilt several times. On November 21,
1906, she survived being run into and sunk by the steam schooner *Cascade* near
Rainer, Washington. The *Lurline* was dismantled in 1931. Her upper works were
still in useable condition. Her cabins and other structures were transferred to the
diesel powered, screw-propelled steamer tug, the *L. P. Hosford*, which stayed in
operation until 1966. The *Lurline* worked for over 50 years, a very long time for a
wooden hulled steamer.

Steamer Manzanillo at Clatskanie, Oregon, in 1885.

(Shaver Transportation Collection)

MANZANILLO: One of Captain James W. Shaver's safest steamers was the *Manzanillo.* This sternwheeler was built in 1881 and was one of the fastest of the smaller steamers on the Columbia River. Captain Shaver worked her on the water for many years. She became a key transport in the family business first called the People's Freighting Company (later known as the Shaver Transportation Company). On the *Manzanillo,* Captain Shaver began hauling freight to the downriver communities as far as Clatskanie, Oregon. Around 1886 or 1887, Captain Shaver sold this steamer to another freighter company. The *Manzanillo* was dismantled in 1893.

MARY: In 1853, this little 80-foot sidewheeler built by Bradford & Company was the first whose wheels churned in the waters of the Columbia River between the Cascades and Lewiston before the Civil War. The *Wasco* followed her in 1855, and then the *Hassalo* in 1857.

During March 26 through the 28th, in 1856, when the Cascade Native Americans battled with new settlers, the *Mary* was docked at the Upper Cascades. Soldiers were stationed at The Dalles 40 miles away and there were no telegraphs. The only hope these terrified settlers had was taking the *Mary* to the soldiers for help. As bullets plummeted through the pilothouse, the volunteer pilot had to huddle by the wheel and steer as signals were called. Little by little, the *Mary* ploughed along, rescuing settlers as she went, until they finally reached their destination. The following morning, both the *Mary* and the *Wasco*, packed with soldiers sent by Colonel Wright, started for the Cascades, where, meeting the troops from another station, rescued the remaining settlers. The *Mary* was dismantled in The Dalles in 1862.

MARY D. HUME: The *Mary D. Hume* was 98-foot long, with a 10-foot depth of hold, and she was 22 feet 8 inches wide. The *Mary D. Hume* was built in Gold Beach (then called Ellensburg), Oregon, in 1881 by R. D. Hume, a pioneer and founder of the Wedderburn community. (Wedderburn was initially a company town for Hume's salmon fishing monopoly, his cannery, racetrack, and cold storage works.) Hume named his steamer after his wife and put her to work to support his cannery operation, spending eight years as a coastal freighter, hauling wool, salmon, and other merchandise from the Oregon coast to San Francisco. In December of 1889, Hume sold her to the Pacific Whaling Company, and she was sent up to Alaska. After passing through several owners and a number of modifications, the *Mary D. Hume* continued to work as late as 1978. She is one of the oldest serving commercial vessels on the West Coast, serving 97 years as a freighter, whaling vessel and as an ocean tugboat. She has never changed her registered name.

An effort was made to preserve the *Mary D. Hume* as a museum ship, but a sling broke when she was being hoisted for repairs, which caused her to slide into the mud at Gold Beach. The *Mary D. Hume* is on the National Register of Historic Places and her remains can still be seen in Gold Beach.

The Mascot is most likely on the lower Columbia River circa 1900.
(Oregon Maritime Museum Collection)

MASCOT: The Lewis & Lake River Company built the *Mascot* in Portland in 1890. The Mascot was the elite sternwheeler on the East Fork, Washington. She had staterooms and a dining room for passengers.

This sternwheeler was 132 feet in length and 267 gross tons. In 1908, she was purchased and rebuilt by Jacob Kamm. Her new length was 141 feet, with a 26-foot 8-inch beam, a 6-foot 8 inch depth of hold, her engines were 13 by 60 inches, and 299 gross tons. She ran the same route as before until 1911 when the steamer was destroyed by fire.

MOUNTAIN BUCK: The *Mountain Buck* was built in Portland in 1857 and was launched June 6. Her first job was running on the Cascade route. She left Portland on July 29, on her first trip with Captain Tom Wright in command and traveled the lower Columbia River to the Cascade Rapids. The *Mountain Buck* met with the *Hassalo* at the Cascades, for passenger journeys up the Columbia River. The *Mountain Buck* was a sidewheeler 133 feet long, with a 25-foot 4-inch beam, and a 5-foot 6-inch hold. She is most noted for being one of the few boats that was originally taken into the Union Transportation Company and the Oregon Steam

147

Navigation Company. With them, the sternwheeler continued on the original route until 1864, when she was stripped of her machinery and left in the boneyard. The *Mountain Buck* was burned in October of 1865.

MULTNOMAH (sidewheeler): The *Multnomah* was one of the first steamboats to run on the Willamette and Yamhill Rivers. She was built in Oregon City, Oregon, on the Willamette River in 1851. She looked very awkward but could make 14 miles an hour and worked on the Willamette River between Oregon City and the Salem area. After 1853, she was used by the People's Line between Oregon City and Portland to the north. At that time, she was considered one of the fastest vessels on the river in the early 1850s, and once was able to travel the 18 miles (29 km) from Portland to Vancouver, Washington, in one hour 20 minutes. In her time, that was a speedy trip. Over the years, her inability to keep up with the other faster and more modern boats left her unused. The *Multnomah* was dismantled in 1865 at Portland.

(Oregon Maritime Museum Collection)

MULTNOMAH (sternwheeler): This *Multnomah* was built for the run from Portland to Oregon City. She was thought to be one of the best boats on the Willamette River. She was built in East Portland, Oregon, in 1885. She worked on both the Columbia and Willamette Rivers until 1889. After that year, she was moved to Puget Sound, Washington. The *Multnomah* was one of the most popular steamers in that region. In 1907, the *Multnomah* was converted from wood to oil-fired boilers. (Almost all the steamboats built after 1905 were oil-fired; they had improved locomotive-style boilers. This reduced the chances of explosion.)

The N. R. Lang on the Willamette River around 1900.
(Oregon Maritime Museum Collection)

N. R. LANG: The passenger and freight steam sternwheeler, the *N. R. Lang* was a rebuilding of a light draft boat built called the *Salem*, built in 1880. The *N. R. Lang* was crafted by Capt. George Raabe in Portland in 1900. She was 528 gross tons and 152 feet in length. She ran from Portland to her homeport in San Francisco. She was dismantled in 1940. The steamer transferred many cargos of paper from the Oregon City paper mills to various locations.

NESTOR: Captain C. P. Stayton and the Ostrander Railway and Timber Company built the *Nestor* in 1902 at Catlin, Washington. Named after Stayton's son, Nestor, she was one of the smallest sternwheelers to work on the Columbia River and its tributary streams. The *Nestor* burned wood for fuel and was often seen with enormous stacks of cordwood carried on her bow. The boat always loaded her wood up at the Menefee Mill in Rainer or at the Ford and Thompson's in West Kelso.

The *Nestor*'s hull was only 82 feet long and 97 gross tons. She spent most of her 27- year life towing log rafts from Ostrander on the Cowlitz River to the old Cowlitz Boom just upstream from the docks along Longview, Washington. Her size gave her a big advantage over other boats as she could glide through the shallow waters with no problems. One of her most noted jobs was towing piling for the construction work for the Lewis & Clark Exposition in Portland in 1905.

Around 1923, her ownership changed over to the Columbia and Cowlitz River Transportation Company, owned jointly by Milton Smith and Ostrander Railway and Timber Company. In 1925, it changed again when Milton Smith took full ownership; he had her rebuilt and converted to oil fuel in Rainer, Oregon. She was dismantled and abandoned near Rainer, Oregon, in 1929.

NEZ PERCE CHIEF: Built in 1863, this sternwheeler was 126 feet and 327 gross tons. She was created specifically for the stretch of the Columbia River that began above the Celilo Falls. Her engines had come from the *Carrie Ladd*, an earlier sternwheeler. Besides her work on the Columbia River, the *Nez Perce Chief* worked along the Snake River up to Lewiston, Idaho, a distance of 141 miles from the mouth of the Snake at Pasco, Washington.

During the gold rush of the 1860s, the *Chief* and other steamboats were key links transporting miners and equipment to the excavating fields and freighting the treasure from the mines out. On one of her trips, she carried out $382,000 worth of gold dust and bars.

In 1870, the *Chief* was transferred to work on the Columbia River between The Dalles and the Cascades near where the town of Cascade Locks is now located. In 1874, she was dismantled in Portland.

This is the damaged bow of the No Wonder in 1889 circa on the Willamette River in Portland, Oregon. (Oregon Maritime Museum Collection)

NO WONDER: In 1897, Shaver Transportation Company bought their fourth boat, the *No Wonder*, which had been built in 1877 by George Washington Wiedler of the Willamette Steam Mills Company, for log towing. She was a 135-foot length, 269 gross ton sternwheeler. (Weidler rebuilt the *Wonder* and renamed her *No Wonder*.) She was the first log towing boat on the Willamette River. The Shaver Transportation Company used *No Wonder* for pulling logs and as a training school for pilots until 1933. The *No Wonder* was dismantled and her hull was left to deteriorate after 56 years of use, which was an exceptional length of time for a wooden hulled steamer.

The sternwheeler, Ocklahama, in 1915, is underway with two sailing ships in a tandem tow on the Columbia River. (Oregon Maritime Museum Collection)

OCKLAHAMA: The *Ocklahama* was built in Portland in 1876 for the Willamette Transportation & Lock Company, only for towing on the Columbia and Willamette Rivers. After its completion, the Oregon Steam Navigation Company purchased it. Her dimensions were: length of 152 feet, a 31-foot 5-inch beam, an 8-foot depth of hold, 582 gross tons, and engines 21 by 72 inches. Captain W. H. Smith first commanded the *Ocklahama*, followed by Captain Henry Emken, Marshall Short, M. Martineau, Kane Olney, and Sam Colson.

Captain Short was killed in 1892 by the capsizing of a barge that the steamer was towing. In 1897, the *Ocklahama* was rebuilt to extend her 9 feet and increase her tons up to 676. She was later abandoned in 1930.

OHIO: The sternwheeler *Ohio* was built in 1874 along the banks of the Willamette River in Portland. Built by U. B. Scott, he named her after where he had learned to steamboat. The *Ohio* was 118 feet between perpendiculars and140 feet overall, with a 24-foot 5-inch beam, 347 gross tons, a 6-foot depth of hold, and an 8-inch draft. Her engines were 10 by 15 inches and had been salvaged from an old dredge. This sternwheeler's gross tonnage was 374 tons. The *Ohio*'s hull was broad and almost flat on the bottom, holding a plain, squarish deckhouse. Lacking enough money, Scott, didn't use iron castings, but framed the wheel from wood and small iron spindles. He had no pitmans, so lengths of gas pipe were used instead.

The *Ohio's* first run was on December 12, 1874; she left the Oregon City Locks, went past Yamhill, Salem, Albany, Corvallis, and Harrisburg, and arrived in Eugene. There she was filled with 70 tons of wheat to take back to Portland. She continued to work, even though her wooden braces occasionally fell loose, or she dropped wheel buckets (leaving the captain to take a skiff out to recover them). In 1881, the *Ohio* was replaced by the steamer *City of Salem*. She was dismantled in Portland, Oregon.

OLYMPIAN: The *Olympian* was a wooden sternwheeler of 154 feet in length with 386 gross tons. She worked as far as the Puget Sound and was one of the last commercial freight steamboats to work on the Columbia River. She was built in 1903 from the wrecked sternwheeler *Telegraph*. Once the single-cylinder engines were compounded, she was placed on the daily Seattle – Olympia - Tacoma run. She was not profitable in this service and was sent down to Portland to work on the Columbia River. There, she was to run a Portland - The Dalles route. Unfortunately, trucks on the newly built Columbia River highway had taken over freight delivery, curtailing the need for riverboats. To keep her in business, the *Olympian's* owners created the practice of roll-on, roll-off hauling. Fully loaded cargo trucks were placed on her deck in Portland and disembarked at the upriver terminal, and then to their final destination. This did not, however, prove to be cost effective. The *Olympian* then ran a brief competition against the speedy *Georgiana* on the Portland - Astoria passenger freight run, but in 1921 was removed from service and laid up in the docks. By 1924, she was left behind by other boats.

ONEONTA: The *Oneonta* was a 150-foot, 497 gross ton sidewheeler built in 1863 in the Cascades by the Oregon Steam Navigation Company that worked on the Columbia River from 1863 to 1877. The *Oneonta* was a Mississippi style steamer with two funnels forward of the pilothouse which was located in the middle of the boat. She worked on the Columbia River between the Cascade Rapids and eastward towards The Dalles and Celilo Falls. The *Oneonta* was the main travel source to run the gold rush between portages along Eastern Oregon and Idaho. Business decreased by 1870, so John C. Ainsworth, her owner, took the *Oneonta* down through the Cascade Rapids to work on the lower Columbia River. By 1877, she was taken out of service and worked as barge until being abandoned in 1880.

ONWARD: The *Onward* was an early sternwheeler built in Canemah on the Willamette River in 1858. (This steamer should not be confused with other vessels named *Onward,* such as the *Onward* built in Colfax, Oregon, in 1867.) This steamer was the successor of the *Enterprise* in Captain Archibald Jamieson's line of vessels. She was built with the proceeds from the sale of the *Enterprise.* She was 125 feet in length, 120 gross tons and very powerful with a large engine and a new locomotive boiler.

Captain Jamieson worked with her until 1860, and then sold her to Jacob Kamm and his business partners. The *Onward* became a great money maker, paying $14,000 in dividends the first year. Kamm was a shareholder in the Oregon Navigation Steam Company and they used this sternwheeler to her full extent. In 1863, the *Onward* was transferred to the People's Transportation Company and Captain George Jerome took command.

When the great flood of the Willamette River occurred in November and December of 1861, it destroyed much of Champoeg and Linn City. The river was filled with wreckage and remains from riverside homes and landings that had been carried away downstream by the flood. The *Onward* could run through the streets of Salem to rescue people. Soon after her rescue, she was dismantled and parted out.

POMONA: The *Pomona* was a steamboat that ran on the Columbia, Cowlitz, and Willamette Rivers, from 1898 to 1940. This sternwheeler was designed to work in low levels of river water. *Pomona* was one of the few steamers that could regularly travel south to Corvallis, Oregon, which was the viable head of navigation on the Willamette. In 1926, *Pomona* was reconstructed and worked as a towboat. In 1940, the *Pomona* was converted into an unpowered floating storehouse.

RAMONA: The sternwheeler *Ramona* was built in Portland, Oregon, in 1892 and was later rebuilt in 1896, enlarged from 100 feet in length to 118. The boat was built for the Graham steamboat line, formally called the Oregon City Transportation Company, but also known as the "Yellow Stack Line." All the steamers of this company had names that ended in -"ona": *Latona, Altona, Leona, Pomona, Oregona,* and *Grahamona.* The *Ramona* was specially tailored for passenger service, and was said to have the best cabins of any steamers operating on the Willamette. She ran from 1892 to 1908 on these rivers: the Willamette in Oregon, the Stikine River from Wrangell, Alaska into British Columbia and the Fraser River in British Columbia. (This is not the same steamship also called the *Ramona,* which ran in the Alaskan waters.)

She worked on the lower Willamette from 1892 to 1894, and then she was transferred to the upper Willamette River (the water above Willamette Falls). For most of this time, Captain A.J. Sprong was in command, with Horace Campbell

154

serving as chief engineer and E. Wynkoop as purser. In 1898, with the coming of the Alaska Gold Rush, the *Ramona* was sent north to run on the Stikine River; there was an effort being made to develop an alternative "All Canadian" route to the Klondike gold fields. *Ramona* was relocated on the Fraser River to replace the steamer *Edgar*. On April 17, 1901, while in service on the Fraser River, the *Ramona*'s boiler exploded, killing at least four people, two women and two deckhands.

The *Ramona* was rescued and repaired after the boiler explosion and returned to service. In October of 1903, the *Ramona* crashed into the Mission railway bridge, but was again repaired and returned to service. Finally, the *Ramona* sank and was left to fade away on April 22, 1908, at Wharton's Landing near the mouth of the Harrison River, British Columbia.

(Oregon Maritime Museum Collection)

REPUBLIC: Built in 1899, in Portland, Oregon, the steam screw passenger boat *Republic* was owned and managed by Captain James Good. She is shown here at Sauvie Island on the Columbia River.

R. R. THOMPSON: Built on the Middle Columbia River and used by the Oregon Steam Navigation Company, the *R. R. Thompson*, named after one of the navigation company's shareholders, was a large sternwheeler steamboat. She was designed in the classic Columbia River style, and was 215 feet in length with a 28-foot beam, a 9 ½-foot depth of hold with 1158 gross tons. Captain J. C. Ainsworth launched her June 1 of 1878. She was then immediately put to work with Captain John McNulty in command and Peter DeHuff as her engineer. She was a fast boat, running from The Dalles to the Cascades (46 miles) in just 2 hours, and then going to Portland at the rate of a mile a minute. The passage of the *R. R. Thompson* through the six mile long Cascade Rapids in 6 minutes 40 seconds was a record that was approached but never beaten.

The *R.R. Thompson* worked in conjunction with the *Wide West,* which carried traffic up to the Cascades from Portland, with stops on the lower river. Once at the Cascades, both the freight and the passengers were moved to the portage railway's cars for a short trip alongside the rapids to the Upper Cascades. From there, the passengers and freight were placed on the *R.R. Thompson,* which ran up the river to The Dalles, where the entire process would be repeated to get through the Celilo Falls.

As the railroads were extended, the *R.R. Thompson* was taken down through the Cascade Rapids on June 3, 1882, by Captain McNulty to run on the more profitable lower Columbia and lower Willamette Rivers. In 1892, she struck a rock near Mt. Coffin, but was raised and brought to Portland for repairs; there she was run as a night boat in Astoria and as a relief boat. Operating as a night boat, her passengers would leave Portland after dinner and arrive in Astoria early the next morning. After a time, she was laid up for several years before she was dismantled in 1904.

SARAH DIXON: The *Sarah Dixon* was built in 1892; she was named after the wife of one founder of Shaver Transportation Company. She was 140 feet in length and 369 gross tons. The *Dixon* had style and elegance; many of her cabins were finished in Birdseye maple. There was even a Birdseye maple piano in the ladies cabin. She was the first of four steamers (the others were *Dalles City, Harvest Queen,* and *Maria*) to go through the Cascade Locks when it opened on November 5, 1896. She became the fastest of the fleet in Portland. The Oregon Railway & Navigation was willing to pay $250 a month to her owners to keep their steamboat off the Portland - Astoria run.

Later, the *Dixon* passed by two steamers on a triumphal parade along the Cascade Locks and arrived in The Dalles a half an hour ahead of the *Regulator.* The irked owners of The Dalles - Portland Navigation Company quickly offered the Shaver Transportation Company $250 a month to get their steamer off their river run. This also happened when she ran from Astoria to Portland and beat the *T. J. Potter* several times. The Oregon Railroad & Navigation Company paid Shaver to keep the *Dixon* off their run.

The *Dixon* was rebuilt in 1906 adding 21 more feet to her length. She worked as a passenger and freight boat, but most of her work was spent in local towing and freight runs between Portland, Clatskanie, and other lower river points. On January 12, 1912, she had the first of two major events that tarnished her 43-year career; it happened on the Kalama River under the command of Captain Fred Stinson. Her boiler exploded and destroyed her upper works, killing Captain Stinson, First Mate Arthur Monica, and Fireman Silas Knowles. The rest of the crew and nine passengers escaped in a small boat. In 1926, she was docked at the Portland Shipbuilding Company when a work barge alongside her caught fire and the flames spread to the *Dixon*. She was rebuilt that same year.

She worked until 1933 when she was dismantled to serve as a floating machine shop. In the mid-1940s this was replaced with an LSM (Landing Ship Medium) and the hull of the *Dixon* was turned over to the Tidewater - Shaver Barge Lines who towed her to Paterson, Washington, on the upper Columbia River and tied up. There her seams opened and she sank and was just left to rust away.

Here in 1906 stand Sarah Shaver, George M. Shaver, Homer T. Shaver, and Nellie Monical in front of the Sarah Dixon.
(Oregon Maritime Museum Collection)

SENORITA: This sidewheeler was originally known as the old *Sarah Hoyt* and was built in Oregon City in 1855. She was 145 feet in length. She was dismantled in 1859.

SHAVER: In 1908, the Shaver Transportation Company manufactured the ordinary 155-foot long steam sternwheeler *Shaver* as a replacement for the old *G.W. Shaver*. The *Shaver* was made at the Portland Shipbuilding Company and included previously used mechanical components from other vessels, such as the steam valves that had served in at least two prior steamboats going back to 1857. Once built, the *Shaver* was used as a tow and workboat until 1927. It was then that her owners converted her into an entirely new technological development: a twin-screw, semi-tunnel diesel tug. Her sternwheel, fantail, and cylinder timbers were all removed. A pair of diesels, set amidships, replaced the engines. Semi-tunnel twin-screw mounts were placed into her hull and propellers fitted into them, giving the *Shaver* an all-new power system. The new *Shaver* was shortened by 24 feet but increased in her gross tons from 368 to 423. From a distance, she looked the same except for the missing sternwheel. She kept her name and continued to work for the Shaver Transportation Company. This new design was used to rebuild the sternwheelers on the Mississippi River in the same way, and new tunnel-screw tugboats there followed this design set by the *Shaver*.

SHUBRICK: The *Shubrick* was just a little sidewheeler that came to the Pacific coast in 1859 to work both as a lighthouse tender and revenue cutter. She was the first, and most likely only, sea going craft to proceed up the Columbia River as far as Ruckel's landing, a short distance above the site for the Bonneville Dam. The *Shubrick* was built in Philadelphia in 1857. She was named after Admiral William Bradford Shubrick, who commanded the Pacific squadron during the Mexican–American War. This sidewheeler served the entire Pacific coast from 1859 until the arrival of the first Manzanita craft (about 1872), and was then transferred to Astoria. The *Shubrick* was later sold at Mare Island navy yard (located 25 miles northeast of San Francisco in Vallejo, California) in 1886 for $3200 and was later dismantled.

STAGHOUND: The sternwheeler *Staghound* had a length of 178 feet 2 inches, a beam of 38 feet, and the engines were 18 ½ by 84 inches high-pressure. She was built for the Yukon Transportation and Commercial Company between 1887 and 1898 in Portland, Oregon. She was to be towed up north to Alaska to work on the Yukon River; unfortunately, she broke her back while being towed across the Columbia River bar. While most of her was salvaged and parts were used for other boats, she was never rebuilt.

STATE OF WASHINGTON: John J. Holland in Tacoma, Washington, built this sternwheeler in 1889. From 1889 to 1902, the *State of Washington* worked on the Seattle - Bellingham route. The following year, she was placed as a standby boat on the Tacoma - Seattle run. Later, she was used on the Hood Canal route. In 1913, the *State of Washington* was moved to the Columbia River under the Shaver Transportation Company. In 1915, she was converted over to a towboat. In 1921, her boiler exploded and six crewmen were injured and one man was killed.

Circa 1900, the Tacoma is on the Columbia River for the Northern Pacific Railroad Company. (Oregon Maritime Museum Collection)

TACOMA: Built in 1884, this iron paddle steamer sidewheel ferry was run by the Northern Pacific Railroad Company for both passengers and freight. Her parts were made in New York and were delivered to Portland by the American Iron sailing ship, the *Tillie E. Starbuck*. Smith Brothers & Watson put her 56,159 pieces together in Portland. The *Tacoma* was 1,362.03 gross tons, with dimensions of 334 feet in length, 42-foot beam, 11.7-foot draft, iron sidewheels, and 76 feet wide. The *Tacoma's* propulsion were two side paddles, each 29 feet in height. She had a capacity of 23 freight cars. She carried 978 feet of rail with a crew of 37 men on board most times.

She was primarily used for transporting trains from Kalama, Washington, on the Columbia River to Hunters Point and Goble, Oregon. The *Tacoma* made her last run on December 25, 1908.

In 1916, she was transferred to Puget Sound and converted into a barge. On January 12, 1950, during a foggy night, now called Barge No. 6, the former *Tacoma* plowed into a ship off Nettleton Point. She sank near Seattle's Elliot bay.

TAHOMA: The sternwheeler *Tahoma* was built in Portland in 1900 for the Vancouver Transportation Company to be used for both freight and passengers on the Portland - Astoria run during the then current rate war. She was named Tahoma in the language of the Yakima and Klickitat Indian tribes, meaning, "the great mountain, which gives thunder and lightning, having unseen powers." This referred to the great Mt. Rainer, overlooking the town of Tacoma, a name that is another spelling of the same mountain. She was 118 feet in length, a 23-foot beam, and a 5 ½-foot depth of hold. She had a gross tonnage of 192 tons, and a net capacity of 146 tons. Her engines were 12 feet by 4 feet, and her boiler pressure was 180 lbs. Both her engines and boiler were rummaged from the sternwheeler *Gov. Newell* that was built in 1883.

The *Tahoma* was used on the Lewis River run for a short time and then spent a few years tied up on the water. She was purchased by the Hosford Transportation Company in 1910 and converted into a towboat for hauling rock barges and log rafts on both the Columbia and Willamette Rivers. In 1912, she was sold to the People's Transportation Company and was used as a freight and passenger steamer on the Portland - The Dalles route. She was then anchored once again until the Shepard Towing Company purchased her and used her to tow log rafts to the McCormick lumber mills at St. Helens, Oregon, until 1929, at which time she was dismantled.

The Telegraph (Larry Barber Collection)

TELEGRAPH: The *Telegraph* was a steel sternwheeler built in 1903 by the Portland Shipbuilding Company in Everett, Washington; she was considered then the fastest sternwheeler in the world. She was 386 gross tons and 154 feet long. The sternwheeler was placed under Capt. U. B. Scott of the Seattle - Everett Navigation Company on the Seattle - Everett route in 1903 to replace the steamer *Greyhound*. In 1910, the Puget Sound Navigation Company bought the *Telegraph*, keeping her on the same route. She worked in Portland for a time in the excursion business during and after the Lewis and Clark Exposition in 1905. On April 25, 1912, the Alaska Steamship Company steel ship *Alameda* hurtled through the Colman Dock in Seattle, striking the *Telegraph* on the other side, almost cutting her in half; she sank within 15 minutes. Amazingly, there was no loss of life. In 1913, the *Telegraph* was sold and renamed the *Olympian*.
She was abandoned in 1924.

TELEPHONE: The *Telephone* was one of the best sternwheeler steamboats ever built; she also went through many changes in her life. She was built in 1885 in Portland. At 172 feet in length, 386 gross tons, she was the fastest boat that plied the northwest waters in the '80s and '90s. On a run between Portland and Astoria one summer day in the '80s, she set a record of four hours and 34 minutes. In 1887, the *Telephone* caught fire along the water's edge. She was rebuilt the next year, adding 28 feet to her length and increasing her capacity up to 500 gross tons. The *Telephone* remained as fast as ever. She was reassembled in 1903. With a new hull, but the upper works from the second *Telephone* that replaced the one burned, the third boat of that name was 202 feet in length and 794 gross tons. She continued to work in Portland until she was transferred to San Francisco Bay for the Western Pacific Railroad in 1909.

TENINO: The *Tenino* was a sternwheeler built by R. R. Thompson and E. F. Coe at the Deschutes River in 1861. She was 135 feet long, a 26-foot beam and had a 5-foot 9-inch depth of hold. Her engines were 17 by 72 inches, constructed by her first engineer, John Gates. She was the second commercial boat on the Columbia River above Celilo Falls and was not only the fastest sternwheeler, but also one of the biggest money makers of the Oregon Steam Navigation Company (OSNC) fleet.

Demand for passage and freight shipments up the Columbia was huge during the early 1860s so the OSNC worked her with the *Colonel Wright*, which was the first steamer they placed above Celilo Falls. The *Tenino* was a bigger and more powerful sternwheeler than her partner. She was run extensively throughout her first few years, but in 1869 was so badly worn out that she had to be rebuilt. Her length was increased by just one extra foot and she was 329 gross tons. She continued to work for another ten years, until in 1876 when she struck a rock while coming down the river, destroying her hull.

She was replaced that year by the *New Tenino*, which was 146 feet long, a 32-foot beam, with 42 gross tons and a 6-foot depth of hold. The *New Tenino*'s engines and house were from the old steamer. Captain T. J. Stump and James W. Troup, with Albert M. Munger as the chief engineer, commanded the steamer. Her short career ended in 1879.

T. J. POTTER: The *T. J. Potter*, commonly referred to as the *Potter*, was named after the first vice president of the Union Pacific Railroad's operations in the west. She was owned by John F. Steffan and launched in Portland in 1888 for the Oregon Railway and Navigation Company.

Her hull was built entirely of wood and was 230 feet long, 659 gross tons, with a beam of 35 feet, and depth of hold of 10½ feet. She was created from the parts of many previous boats. Her upper cabins came from the steamboat *Wide West*, which required some modification, since the *T.J. Potter* had been a sidewheeler, while the *Wide West* was a sternwheeler. She was driven by two noncondensing steam engines with 32-inch cylinders, each with an 8-foot stroke, generating around 1,700 horsepower. Her single boiler was 32 feet long with a diameter of 84 inches. The Pusey & Jones Company of Wilmington, Delaware, built both the boiler and the firebox in 1887. Her gross tonnage was 659 and her net tonnage was 589.

Captain James W. Troup, a distinguished steamboat captain in the northwest, as well as the owner of the Oregon Railway and Navigation Company, supervised the building of the *T. J. Potter*. Once she was launched, the *Potter* had a reputation as one of the fastest and most luxurious steamboats in the Pacific Northwest.

On her very first season, her owners put her on the 105-mile tourist run from Portland to Astoria. In August of 1888, she made that run in only 5 hours and 31 minutes. By comparison, the fastest steamboat on the Columbia River at that time was the *Potter*'s competitor, the *Telephone*, which on July 2, 1887, made the same run in 4 hours and 34 minutes.

Fares were $2.50 to Astoria and $3.00 to Ilwaco, Washington. Discounts were offered for the round trip. Lower berths cost $.75 and a single berth cost $.50. All meals cost $.50.

The *T. J. Potter* was rebuilt in 1901, increasing her length by 4 feet and her gross tons to 1017. She was removed as a tourist boat in 1916. She then served as a barracks boat for construction crews until November 20, 1920. Her license was revoked and she was left on Young's Bay near Astoria. Shortly afterward, she was burned and salvaged for her metal. The *Potter* has heavily deteriorated over the past 80 years. All that remains are parts of most of the ribs as well as the keel. The starboard paddle box remains but the wheels are believed to have been removed.

UMATILLA: This sternwheeler was built in 1908 in Celilo, Oregon. The U.S. Army Corps of Engineers rebuilt her in 1928. In her later years, the Shaver Transportation Company owned her and used her for towing. She was dismantled in 1942.

(Larry Barber Collection)

UNDINE: Built by Jacob Kamm in 1888, she was 150 feet in length with a 27-foot beam, 16.4 by 60 inches engines, and a 6-foot hold. The *Undine* was used on a Vancouver route, with occasional trips to Astoria and in business trips. She normally made two round trips a day on the Vancouver route. Captain Charles T. Kamm was in charge until 1892, when Joseph Burgy took command. Here she is, first in line from Portland to go to Lewiston, Idaho, during the week-long celebrations of the opening of The Dalles – Celilo Locks and Canal celebration. The *Undine* was the flagship to a long line of ships and boats participating in these festivities

VENTURE: The *Venture* was a little wooden steamer sternwheeler built by R. R. Thompson in Collins, across from the Cascades, in 1858 for the run to The Dalles. She was 110 feet in length with a 22-foot beam, 14 by 48 inches engines, and 91 gross tons. On her maiden voyage, she started out with a low head of steam and 40 passengers. When the *Venture* got out into the river, the current carried her backwards and swept her stern first over the rapids, where she landed on a rock. Captain E. W. Baughman, who later became well known along the river, was close by with his small schooner. He rescued the passengers, excepting one man who got so distressed, he jumped overboard, never to be found. The *Venture* was later raised and renamed the *Umatilla,* which served on the lower Columbia until 1858.

WASCO: This little sidewheeler was launched in 1855 in the Cascades, Washington. She was built by Bradford & Company and worked with the *Mary* on the waters of the Columbia River between the Cascades and Lewiston before the Civil War. The *Hassalo* soon followed her in 1857.

The evening of March 26, 1856, when the Cascade Native Americans battled with new settlers, the *Wasco* was docked at the Upper Cascades. Colonel Wright loaded his troops on both the *Mary* and the *Wasco*. Col. Wright ordered a flatboat lined to the *Wasco* with their supplies. The towed flatboat was difficult to manage, and the sidewheeler had barely enough power, even helped with the current, to keep ahead of the barge and keep it in the right direction. By the night of the 27th, Col. Wright's soldiers had covered less than half the fifty-two miles to the Cascades when both boats had to tie up at the bank. Morning broke and the steamers crossed over to the Oregon bank, where the men dispersed with their supplies. The *Wasco* continued to work until 1861.

WEOWN: The sternwheeler *Weown* was built in 1907 in Portland by the St. Johns Shipbuilding Company yards for the Columbia and Cowlitz River Transportation Company. Her length was 153 feet and 372 gross tons. She had a 31 ½-foot beam, with a 6 ½-foot depth of hold, and a draft of 4 ½ feet. She was built with the sternwheeler *Regulator'*s engines that were 72 by 16 inches. Her firebox boiler was 225 pounds steam pressure. She was launched in June, and was used for towing logs on both the Columbia and Willamette Rivers.

On June 17, 1933, the *Weown* became the last sternwheeler to run the Cascade Rapids. In February of 1908, she was sold to Hosford Transportation Company. They used her until 1934, when Shaver Transportation bought her. After working the waters for four more years, the *Weown* was dismantled in 1936. By 1938, her hull was left abandoned.

WIDE WEST: The Oregon Steam & Navigation Company built the *Wide West* in 1877 in Portland. This lavish sternwheeler was of wood construction, 218 feet, 39 ½-foot beam, 8-foot depth of hold, 28 by 96 inches engine and was 1200 gross tons. The *Wide West* was placed under the command of Captain Wolf. She had occasional trips to Astoria, but mostly ran the Portland - Cascade run for several years. Passengers would have to disembark and ride a short railway around the Cascades to board another steamboat to travel further upriver. Cargo would have to be unloaded and reloaded again. No one objected to the awkward travel as the

Wide West had a reputation as a luxury boat for her time. In 1880, the *Wide West* made a trip to Astoria from Portland in only 5 hours.

Over her time, Captains Babbidge, Clarke W. Sprague, and A. B. Pittsbury were also in command of this steamer. In 1887, she was taken to the bone yard; her house and most of her fittings were transferred to the new sidewheeler *T. J. Potter*. The hull was sold to Puget Sound interests, who equipped her with a small engine. She was then sent up to Washington, where she wrecked on Destruction Island in 1899.

The steamer William M. Hoag was sunk at the upper end of the Willamette Falls Locks in Oregon City.   (Oregon Maritime Museum Collection)

WILLIAM M. HOAG: *William M. Hoag* was a steamer built in 1887 in East Portland. She was used as a feeder for the Oregon Pacific Coast Railroad Co. At 452 tons, thirty-two feet beam, 16 x 72 engines producing 17 horsepower, and 150-foot length, she was manned by Captain George Raabe until 1892. She was then turned over to Captains Robert Young and Miles Bell. In 1903, she was rebuilt to become the steamer *Annie Comings*. As the *Annie Comings*, she collided with the French wheat bark *Europe* and sunk at the upper end of the Willamette Falls Locks on the Oregon City side in 1907. This boat was rebuilt again in 1909 and finally dismantled in 1941.

YAKIMA: In 1864, the sternwheeler steamer *Yakima* was completed in Celilo and made her trial trip May 4, under Captain Charles Felton. She was launched on the Upper Columbia River to Celilo Falls, and then on to the Snake River. The *Yakima* was a beautiful steamer with 26 gracefully furnished staterooms. She was 137 feet long with a 29-foot beam, 455 gross tons, 5-foot depth of hold, and engines 17 by 72 inches.

In June of 1867, under Captain E. F. Coe, she set a record 41½ hours from Celilo to Lewiston, a distance of 279 miles, against a very fast current and with many rapids to climb; it has never been outdone. Captain Coe commanded the *Yakima* until 1870, when Captain Thomas Stump, the last master of the *Yakima*, succeeded him. In 1876, while on her way down the river with one hundred and sixty tons of freight, she crashed into a rock in the John Day Rapids. It tore into the bottom and pushed nearly past the boiler, causing her to sink in shallow water. This was not the *Yakima*'s first disaster, but was of such a serious nature that she was of very little value after she was raised. A second *Yakima* sternwheeler was built in Ainsworth, Washington, in 1906. This boat was also 137 feet in length but was just 393 gross tons. She was deserted in 1924.

APPENDIX D: THE SHAVER TRANSPORTATION COMPANY

The Shaver Transportation Company is still on the waters in Portland.

George W. Shaver founded the Shaver Transportation Company as a family owned business. In 1880, Mr. Shaver and his partners developed the People's Freighting Company. Their first vessel was the steamboat *Manzanilla*, which they worked on the Willamette and Columbia Rivers between Portland and Clatskanie, Oregon. In 1893, Shaver and his sons James W. Shaver and George M. Shaver created Shaver Transportation. Their next two steam-powered sternwheelers were the *George W. Shaver* and the *Sarah Dixon*, named for his wife. Shaver soon moved away from transporting people and cargo, preferring to work in barge towing, and the fleet grew to seven tugs by 1914.

By 1950, Shaver Transportation had two-dozen steel-hulled diesel engine tugs. Log towing was a large portion of the business during these years. In addition, Shaver established itself in ship assist work in Portland's booming harbor and in ocean towing up and down the coast from Alaska to the Panama Canal.

For five generations, the Shaver family continues hands-on management and ownership of the company. Harry Shaver is Chairman of the Board. His son, Steve Shaver, is President of the company and worked on the tugs for over seventeen years, thirteen of those as a captain. He also worked with the Columbia River Pilots for a short time. Steve soon returned to his family's business. Harry's daughter, Samantha Shaver, is a Member of the Board. The company currently has about 90 employees. Today, Shaver Transportation focuses on three lines of business: ship assist, grain barging, and harbor/specialty towing.

http://www.shavertransportation.com/index.html

The G. W. Shaver and the Sarah Dixon in 1896. (Shaver Transportation)

BIBLIOGRAPHY

Affleck, Edward L., compiled. <u>A Century of Paddlewheelers in the Pacific Northwest, the Yukon, and Alaska</u>. Alexander Nicolls Press. Vancouver, B.C. 2000.

Bagley, Clarence. <u>History of Seattle from the Earliest Settlement to the Present Time, Volume 2.</u> Nabu Press. Charleston, South Carolina. 2010.

Corning, Howard McKinley. "Other Landings of a Bygone Day." <u>Willamette Landings</u>. 1947. Portland Historical Society. Seattle, Washington. 2004. 169-180.

John, Finn J. D. <u>Wicked Portland: the Wild and Lusty Underworld of a Frontier Seaport Town</u>. History Press. Charleston, South Carolina. 2012.

Mills, Randall V. <u>Stern-wheelers Up Columbia: A Century of Steamboating in the Oregon Country</u>. 1947. University of Nebraska Press. Lincoln, Nebraska. 1977.

Timmen, Fritz. <u>Blow for the Landing: A Hundred Years of Steam Navigation on the Waters of the West</u>. Caxton Printers, Ltd. Caldwell, Idaho. 1973.

Wilson, Fred W. <u>Steamboat Days on the Rivers</u>. Oregon Historical Society. Portland, Oregon. 1969.

Winther, Oscar O. "The Coming of Paddlewheels." <u>Old Oregon Country; A History of Frontier Trade, Transportation, and Travel.</u> Stanford University Press. Stanford, California.1950. 157-173.

Wright, E. W., editor. <u>Lewis and Dryden's Marine History of the Pacific Northwest: an Illustrated Review of the Growth and Development of the Maritime Industry, from the Advent of the Earliest Navigators to the Present Time, with Sketches and Portraits of a Number of Well Known Marine Men.</u> 1895. Seattle, Superior Publishing Co., Seattle, Washington.1967.

Building the Portland. n.d. In *Oregon Maritime Museum*. Retrieved 2014-15 from http://www.oregonmaritimemuseum.org/history.html

Columbia River. n.d. In *The Columbia River - A Photographic Journey*. Retrieved June, 2014 from http://columbiariverimages.com/index.html

Hassalo sternwheeler. n.d. In *Wikipedia*. Retrieved July 2014 from http://en.wikipedia.org/wiki/Hassalo_%28sternwheeler_1880%29

James Miller. n.d. In *Wikipedia*. Retrieved February 2016 from https://en.wikipedia.org/wiki/James_D._Miller

Magellan – The Ships Navigator. n.d. In *Cimorelli*. Retrieved April 2015 from http://www.cimorelli.com/magellan/

Northwest Harbors & Seaports. n.d. In *The Maritime Heritage Project*. Retrieved April 2014 from http://www.maritimeheritage.org/ports/usWashington.html

Paddle Steamers. n.d. In *Wikipedia*. Retrieved March 2014 from http://en.wikipedia.org/wiki/Paddle_steamer.

Portland (steam tug). n.d. In *Wikipedia*. Retrieved 2014 from http://en.wikipedia.org/wiki/Portland_%28steam_tug_1947%29.

Wooden Boats. n.d. In *Bellingham Maritime Museum*. Retrieved September 2014 from http://www.bellinghammaritimemuseum.org/exhibit/

I would like to thank these organizations for their assistance and for giving me full access to their records:

Clackamas County Family History Society Wilmer Gardner Research Library, Museum of the Oregon Territory, 211 Tumwater Dr., Oregon City, Oregon, 97045, USA

Oregon Maritime Museum, 115 SW Ash St, Suite 400C, Portland, Oregon, 97204, USA

Veteran Steamboatmen's Association of the West, 10235 SE Stephens St., Portland OR 97216, USA

Sternwheeler Portland being restored by Oregon Maritime Museum

Made in the USA
San Bernardino, CA
05 August 2016